Shakespeare on the Shades of Racism examines Shakespeare in relation to ongoing conversations that interrogate the vulnerability of Black and brown people amid oppressive structures that aim to devalue their worth. By focusing on the way these individuals are racialized, politicized, policed, and often violated in our contemporary world, it casts light on dimensions of Shakespeare's work that afford us a better understanding of our ethical responsibilities in the face of such brutal racism.

Shakespeare on the Shades of Racism is divided into seven short chapters that cast light on contemporary issues regarding racism in our day. Some salient topics that these chapters address include the murder of unarmed Black men and women, the militarization of the U.S. Mexico border, anti-immigrant laws, exclusionary measures aimed at Syrian refugees, inequities in healthcare and safety for women of color, international trends that promote white nationalism, and the dangers of complicity when it comes to racist paradigms. By bringing these contemporary issues into conversation with a wide range of plays that span the many genres in which Shakespeare wrote throughout his career, these chapters demonstrate how the widespread racism and discord within our present moment stands to infuse with urgent meaning Shakespeare's attention to the (in)humanity of strangers, the ethics of hospitality, the perils of insularity, abuses of power, and the vulnerability of the political state and its subjects.

The book puts into conversation Shakespeare with present-day events and cultural products surrounding topics of race, ethnicity, xenophobia, immigration, asylum, assimilation, and nationalism as a means of illuminating Shakespeare's cultural and literary significance in relation to these issues. It should be an essential read for all students of literary studies and Shakespeare.

Ruben Espinosa is Associate Professor of English at the University of Texas, El Paso, U.S.A.

Spotlight on Shakespeare

Series Editors: John Garrison and Kyle Pivetti

Spotlight on Shakespeare offers a series of concise, lucid books that explore the vital purchase of the modern world on Shakespeare's work. Authors in the series embrace the notion that emergent theories, contemporary events, and movements can help us shed new light on Shakespeare's work and, in turn, his work can help us better make sense of the contemporary world. The aim of each volume is two-fold: to show how Shakespeare speaks to questions in our world and to illuminate his work by looking at it through new forms of human expression. *Spotlight on Shakespeare* will adopt fresh scholarly trends as contemporary issues emerge, and it will continually prompt its readers to ask, "What can Shakespeare help us see? What can he help us do?"

Spotlight on Shakespeare invites scholars to write non-exhaustive, pithy studies of very focused topics—with the goal of creating books that engage scholars, students, and general readers alike.

Available in this series:

Shakespeare at Peace
John Garrison and Kyle Pivetti

Shakespeare and Queer Representation
Stephen Guy-Bray

Shakespeare on the Shades of Racism
Ruben Espinosa

For more information about this series, please visit: www.routledge.com/Spotlight-on-Shakespeare/book-series/SOSHAX

RUBEN ESPINOSA

Shakespeare
on the Shades
of Racism

Routledge
Taylor & Francis Group

LONDON AND NEW YORK

First published 2021
by Routledge
2 Park Square, Milton Park, Abingdon, Oxon OX14 4RN

and by Routledge
605 Third Avenue, New York, NY 10158

Routledge is an imprint of the Taylor & Francis Group, an informa business

British Library Cataloguing-in-Publication Data
A catalogue record for this book is available from the British Library

Library of Congress Cataloging-in-Publication Data
A catalog record has been requested for this book

ISBN: 978-0-367-18299-1 (hbk)
ISBN: 978-0-367-18300-4 (pbk)
ISBN: 978-0-429-06061-8 (ebk)

Typeset in Joanna
by Newgen Publishing UK

For Andrea

Contents

Acknowledgments

I am deeply grateful to the *Spotlight on Shakespeare* series editors, John Garrison and Kyle Pivetti, not only for inviting me to work on this book but also for their unending patience as I struggled to meet my deadlines (yes, that is plural). Their support, understanding, and overall goodwill kept me moving forward, even when I thought I would not be able to bring this project to completion. Thank you. I am also grateful to Polly Dodson at Routledge for believing in this.

I feel fortunate to belong to the supportive group of scholars who make up the ShakeRace community. There are too many of you to name, but you know who you are, and I am deeply grateful to you. This community has provided an intellectual home for me, and that has made all the difference. I am indebted to the following friends and colleagues who have read, commented on, and/or afforded me opportunities to present on the material from this book, especially because I find their work so inspiring: Michelle Dowd, Farah Karim-Cooper, Emily King, Peggy O'Brien, Kathryn Vomero Santos, Ian Smith, and Ayanna Thompson. Ayanna, in particular, has a pronounced influence on my thinking and career path, and I admire her tremendously because she consistently reminds us all why this work matters. She is a mentor to a generation of scholars that will change our field for the better. Of most importance, she has been an incredibly good friend to me.

Three symposia had a particularly influential effect on my thinking, and the many participants at those events inspired various aspects of this book: The "Shakespeare and Race" Symposium at Shakespeare's Globe in 2018, the Keefe Colloquium in the Humanities at Lafayette College in 2019, and the RaceB4Race Symposium in Washington, D.C. in 2019. The conversations that these events engendered shaped the way I envisioned this project, but beyond the inspiration those conversations offered, I am simply grateful that I was able to think with the following individuals: Patricia Akhimie, Dennis Britton, David Sterling Brown, Jonathan Burton, Urvashi Chakravarty, Kim Coles, Ambereen Dadabhoy, Peter Erickson, Katherine Gillen, Miles Grier, Kim F. Hall, Margo Hendricks, Arthur Little, Joyce Green MacDonald, Erika Lin, Carol Mejia LaPerle, and Debapriya Sarkar. Because of the people involved, I will forever remember these events fondly.

My parents are the reason I have the confidence to do this work, and it isn't lost on me how hard they worked to give me the opportunity to choose this path. Their fingerprints are on everything worthwhile that I do. My siblings, Armando, Elizabeth and Connie, their spouses, and my many nieces and nephews have always been supportive of my work, and I am so very grateful to them. To my kids, Sophia and Marcello, I love you and I am consistently proud of you. Thank you especially, Marcello, for reading my work and pretending that you think it's cool.

Madelyn and Alex Shaheen, Alexis and Kyle Gorham, Sarah Sultan and Christopher Shaheen—and my nieces, Ella, Adrienne, and Charlie—have enlivened my world in such significant ways. At every turn, they have shown genuine kindness and goodwill, and I feel so incredibly fortunate to be a part of this family.

In the process of writing this book, my son Mathéo grew into the four-year-old toddler he is now. He is the absolute best distraction to writing. My youngest son, Emilián, came into this world at that tail-end of this project, and he showed zero regard for my deadline. In a year that has felt impossible, he consistently reminds me that the world and its goodness is bigger than us. As I write this, he is asleep beside me. I have thoroughly loved burning the midnight oil with him by my side.

My students at UTEP keep me on my toes and are all too often the recipients of my underdeveloped ideas. Always, they make me better. To all of my colleagues in the Department of English at UTEP, thank you. Brian Yothers, Chair of the Department of English, and Denis O'Hearn, Dean of Liberal Arts at UTEP, have encouraged the direction of my work without reservation and with genuine excitement. For that, I am grateful. My close friends at (or formerly at) UTEP, Sasha Pimentel, Michael Topp, Chuck Ambler, Joe Ortiz, and Ezra Cappell, always bring joy, irreverence, and laughter into my life. They are my people, and that is my good fortune. Hands down, though, my favorite person at UTEP is Andrea Shaheen Espinosa.

To say that Andrea has influenced this book is a vast understatement that altogether ignores the profoundly positive effect she has had on every single facet of my life. I love to think with her, I love that she is the one beside me when I feel the weight of this world, and I love that her voice is always with me. Above all, I love her. I dedicate this book to you, Andrea, because the moment you entered into my life, everything was suddenly meaningful in a way I did not think was possible. I have a hundred books in me because of you, and because of you, I want to write them all.

Introduction: Vulnerable bodies

When Hamlet's clever wordplay leads Polonius to abandon his conversation with the eponymous hero, the audience is presented with a line that ostensibly holds universal appeal. Frustrated with Hamlet's enigmatic answers, Polonius says to him, "My lord, I will take my leave of you," to which Hamlet responds, "You cannot take from me anything that I will not more willingly part withal—except my life, except my life, except my life" (2.2.233–5).[1] With striking gravity, Hamlet lays bare a vulnerability that every one of us confronts, as one's life can be taken at any moment. But some lives, we know, are rendered more vulnerable than others. Because Hamlet so often exists as a model of identification for readers and critics—and because race in *Hamlet* is often ignored so as to enable "the normative invisibility of whiteness,"[2] as Ian Smith has provocatively argued—it becomes that much more vital for us to consider how the concept of vulnerable bodies changes meaning when we take into account the experiences of those dark of skin. In doing so, we find that Hamlet's repetitive statement holds both a greater and a more ominous valence. If we imagine Hamlet as Black, the full weight of these words is there for us to behold.

This book takes to heart the fundamental understanding that Black lives matter less in the minds of many within our contemporary society, and it interrogates how confronting and engaging structures of racism stands to infuse Shakespeare's work with a currency that is vital in our present moment. It asks us to consider not only how the notion of vulnerability is magnified for Black and brown people but also the way that very vulnerability enkindles white anger and helps to sustain structures of white supremacy. I have in mind here Carol Anderson's sharp critique of media narratives that perpetuate perceptions of "black rage" in our society when Black communities react to racist paradigms that result in the violent acts against Black Americans, more often than not at the hands of law enforcement officials. The true rage at work, she argues, is a sinister white rage that is not always visible, but one that permeates the fabric of our society.[3] What Anderson identifies as the "trigger for white rage" is the threat of Black advancement and the idea that Black people stand to demand "full and equal citizenship."[4] The significance of this for Black people is obvious, but it is Anderson's attention to the enduring vulnerabilities of whiteness—the tenuous hold it has on justifying its perceived superiority—that I find compelling. The very idea that a demand for equal citizenship is deemed threatening enough to engender white rage signals the enduring belief that Black individuals are imagined as lesser than those white of skin. It opens the door to the dehumanization of Black people.

This dehumanization, of course, extends far beyond the Black individuals in our contemporary society, and we witness this vividly in anti-immigrant sentiments within the United States. For this reason, this book extends its attention to racism to consider Black and brown people. The idea of brown individuals stands to encapsulate an array of people from a variety of racial and ethnic identities, but admittedly, my use of the term is mostly limited to dark-skinned Latinxs. Even this narrower focal point, though, is problematic, as the varied identities encapsulated in the Latinx label are hardly uniform, and I am vividly aware of this fact even as I employ it as an umbrella term. While I sometimes draw attention to experiences of other people of color throughout the book, my emphasis—for the sake of manageability—will focus on Black and Latinx experiences. I want to make it absolutely clear that in no way is my intent to conflate Black and Latinx histories or experiences, but rather my aim is to locate through the varied experiences a sense of solidarity that cuts across color lines in an effort to challenge racist ideologies and white supremacy.

As James Baldwin, Ta-Nehisi Coates, Kimberlé Crenshaw, Angela Davis, Frantz Fanon, bell hooks, and a host of others have deftly argued, the Black experience is one wrought with the threat of tyranny and violence at every turn.[5] Although distinctly different in regard to historical circumstances and forms of oppression, the experiences of "expendability and exploitability" for Blacks and Latinxs are similar.[6] To be certain, these experiences of oppression are germane to many colonized and formerly colonized peoples, and this book keeps that in mind even as it delimits, out of necessity, its critical scope. In many ways, though, the hope is that the foci of this book will influence studies that extend beyond the brown individuals that I discuss here.

As I put these issues into conversation with Shakespeare, I take to heart Ayanna Thompson's argument that, "to engage contemporary notions of Shakespeare, race, and universalism, one must be attuned to a wider variety of sources: one must be willing to engage in cultural studies in the broadest sense."[7] To that end, I draw on journalistic, filmic, dramatic, musical, and varied forms of cultural artifacts that speak to the vulnerability of Black and brown people. Considering such artifacts alongside Shakespeare and adaptations/appropriations of his works enkindles provocative understandings of present-day issues surrounding social and racial inequities that render vulnerable so many Black and brown individuals—a vulnerability on which *Shakespeare on the Shades of Racism* squarely casts light. As such, the shades to which this book's title alludes are vitalized in ways that ask us to consider the various facets behind structures of racism in earnest.

Putting Shakespeare into conversation with contemporary understandings of racism is likely to elicit scrutiny, as the argument often goes that early modern England had a vastly different understanding of race than we do in the present and, as such, arguments of anachronism are often strategically deployed to undermine studies focused on race. My unvarnished take on this is that such views regarding race and early modern literature are facile and idle ways to evade not necessarily the topic of race but the topic of racism. In no uncertain terms, it is the issue of racism that I aim to take up in this book. To get there, then, I want to offer a few definitions and perspectives regarding race both in early modernity and in the present moment that will guide my thinking.

The contributions of Geraldine Heng to understanding European premodern racial formations cannot be overstated. Heng's lucid tracing of the way race was imagined through an array of sources in medieval Europe long before we possessed a vocabulary for race offers a compelling entry point to interrogating what we talk about when we talk about race in pre- and early modern studies. In discussing the "locations of medieval race," Heng writes:

> I begin with a modest working hypothesis: that "race" is one of the primary names we have—a name we retain precisely for the strategic, epistemological, and political commitments

it recognizes—attached to a repeating tendency, of the gravest import, to demarcate human beings through difference among humans that are selectively essentialized as absolute and fundamental, in order to distribute positions and powers differentially to human groups. Racial formation therefore occurs as specific historical occasions in which strategic essentialisms are posited and assigned through a variety of practices and pressures, so as to construct a hierarchy of peoples for differential treatment. My understanding, thus, is that *race is a structural relationship for the articulation and management of human differences, rather than a substantive content.*[8]

In arriving at the constructed hierarchy that posits social inequities based on difference, Heng highlights the stakes behind such demarcation of human beings. The workings of race are meant to keep certain individuals in the shadows of others. Absent of "substantive content," race is not tethered to anything remotely stable.

Because of Heng's thoughtful articulation about racial formations in the pre- and early modern world, we can indeed interrogate the term "race" from our present standpoint despite the perception that anachronistic understandings of the term fall short since "race" was not a stable concept in the early modern period. As Vanessa Corredera argues, our own racial discourses "depend on and perpetuate an understanding of race no less fluid than the racial discourses of early modernity."[9] Race now, like then, is vastly unstable. Barbara and Karen Fields explain:

Race is not an element of human biology (like breathing oxygen or reproducing sexually); nor is it even an idea (like the speed of light or the value of π) that can be plausibly imagined to live an eternal life of its own. Race is not an idea but an ideology. It came into existence at a discernible historical moment for rationally understandable historical reasons and is subject to change for similar reasons.[10]

Those reasons, as Fields and Fields note, have to do with structures of inequality—the very structures that were used to justify slavery in America. Race, then, is mobilized at various historical moments, including our own, to sustain an imbalance of power and oppressive structures that always favor whiteness.

The seeming neutrality of whiteness, an often-ignored shade of race, speaks volumes about the level of inequality and about the racism that surrounds the ideology of race. While perceptions of difference that include, but certainly are not limited to, phenotype, language, and religion govern racial discourses, whiteness is often omitted from the equation. As Robin DiAngelo argues at the onset of her study of white fragility, "White people in North America live in a society that is deeply separate and unequal by race, and white people are the beneficiaries of that separation and inequality."[11] As a result of this inequality, DiAngelo says, whites "are insulated from racial stress, at the same time that we come to feel entitled to and deserving of our advantage."[12] This is quite similar to what George Lipsitz describes as the "possessive investment in whiteness" that renders so many complicit in a system that perpetuates significant social inequities.[13] Always, this system favors whiteness.

The resulting racism that emerges within a society that fosters such inequalities is the topic that this book seeks to interrogate, and it uses Shakespeare as a vehicle to do so. In so many ways, Shakespeare embodies whiteness and exists as a cultural icon that many aspire to access. Unsurprisingly, the ambitions of people of color who seek to access Shakespeare—actors, dramaturgs, critics, scholars, and students alike—are often trivialized. Quite often, people of color are made to feel that their renditions, adaptations, readings, and understandings of Shakespeare are inauthentic, and that, in many ways, Shakespeare does not belong to them. In my brown skin, I'm here to tell you that what they actually mean to say when they suggest that Shakespeare does not belong to us is that *we* simply don't belong. I want to make it clear that we do indeed belong, and to make clear that looking at Shakespeare with the darker shades of racism of our present moment in mind is necessary to preserving his vitality in our day.

It is in that vein that this book attempts to engage Shakespeare not only to see what his works offer in the way of understanding the various forms of racism in our present moment, but to see how the various forms of racism in our present moment allow us to reconceive of Shakespeare's value anew. Some salient topics that the chapters in this book address include the murder of unarmed Black people, the militarization of the U.S. Mexico border, anti-immigrant laws, exclusionary measures aimed at refugees, inequities in healthcare and safety for women of color, disenfranchisement of people of color, and international trends that promote white nationalism. By bringing these contemporary issues into conversation with a wide range of plays that span the many genres in which Shakespeare wrote throughout his career, the chapters that follow seek to demonstrate how Shakespeare's attention to the humanity of strangers, the urgency of hospitality, the perils of insularity, abuses of power, implicit and explicit racism, and the vulnerability of the political state and its subjects affords us a more meaningful understanding of the discord within our present moment. But I also want to make clear that I am not looking to Shakespeare to see what he can teach us about these issues, nor do I hesitate to find moments in and through Shakespeare where racist structures are perpetuated. I want these issues to inform the way we engage with the works of Shakespeare. Of most import-ance, perhaps, this book puts the spotlight on the undeniable importance of those people of color who have contributed, and who continue to contribute, meaningfully, invaluably, and unflaggingly to our contemporary society.

NOTES

1 William Shakespeare, *Hamlet*, ed. Barbara Mowat and Paul Werstine. (New York: Folger Shakespeare Library, 2012). All citations of Shakespeare are to act, scene, and line number.

2 Ian Smith, "We are Othello: Speaking of Race in Early Modern Studies," *Shakespeare Quarterly* 67.1 (2016), 107.

3 Carol Anderson, *White Rage: The Unspoken Truth of Our Racial Divide* (New York: Bloomsbury, 2016), 3.

4 Ibid, 3.

5 See, for example: James Baldwin, *Notes of a Native Son* (Boston: Beacon Press, 1955); Ta-Nehisi Coates, "The First White President," *The Atlantic*, October 2017; Kimberlé Crenshaw, "Unmasking Colorblindness in the Law: Lessons from the Formation of Critical Race Theory," *Seeing Race Again: Countering Colorblindness Across the Disciplines*, ed. Kimberlé Crenshaw, Luke Charles Harris, Daniel Martinez HoSang, and George Lipsitz (Oakland, CA: U of California P, 2019), 52–84; Angela Davis, *Freedom Is a Constant Struggle: Ferguson, Palestine, and the Foundations of a Movement* (Chicago: Haymarket Books, 2016); Frantz Fanon, *Black Skin, White Masks* (New York: Grove Press, 1952); and bell hooks, *Killing Rage: Ending Racism* (New York: Holt and Company, 1995).

6 John Márquez, "Juan Crow: Progressive Mutations of the Black-White Binary," *Critical Ethnic Studies: A Reader*, ed. Nada Elia, et al. (Durham NC: Duke UP, 2016), 48.

7 Ayanna Thompson, *Passing Strange: Shakespeare, Race, and Contemporary America* (Oxford: Oxford UP, 2011), 43.

8 Geraldine Heng, "The Invention of Race in the European Middle Ages II: Locations of Medieval Race," *Literature Compass* 8.5 (2011), 332.

9 Vanessa Corredera, "'Not a Moor exactly': Shakespeare, *Serial*, and Modern Constructions of Race," *Shakespeare Quarterly* 67.1 (2016), 33. For more on the conversation surrounding the reluctance of scholars to see similarities in modern and early modern constructions of race, see: Kim F. Hall, *Things of Darkness: Economies of Race and Gender in Early Modern England* (Ithaca, NY: Cornell UP, 1995); Sujata Iyengar, *Shades of Difference: Mythologies of Skin Color in Early Modern England* (Philadelphia: U of Pennsylvania, 2005); Arthur Little, *Shakespeare Jungle Fever: National-Imperial Re-Visions of Race, Rape, and Sacrifice* (Stanford, CA: Stanford UP, 2000); and Ayanna Thompson, *Passing Strange*.

10 Barbara Fields and Karen Fields, *Racecraft: The Soul of Inequality in American Life* (London: Verso, 2012), 121.

11 Robin DiAngelo, *White Fragility: Why It's So Hard for White People to Talk About Racism* (Boston: Beacon Press, 2018). 1.

12 Ibid., 1.

13 George Lipsitz, *The Possessive Investment in Whiteness: How White People Profit from Identity Politics* (Philadelphia: Temple UP, 1998), 233.

One

Billie Holiday's haunting song "Strange Fruit" poignantly captures the horror of our history of violence against Blacks in the United States. She steadily sings of the lynched Black people hanging from trees as "fruit for crows to pluck / For the rain to gather, for the wind to suck / For the sun to rot, for the trees to drop / Here is a strange and bitter crop."[1] The juxtaposition of her soulful voice against the horrific image of rotting Black bodies induces something deeply unsettling. And we should be unsettled. Indeed, in our recent history, we have borne witness to this "strange and bitter" fruit scattered throughout our nation's landscape. Tanisha Anderson, Michael Brown, Philando Castile, Amadou Diallo, Eric Garner, Freddie Gray, Eric Harris, Kendra James, Tamir Rice—all Black, all unarmed, and all unjustly murdered by the police. The images of Black violated bodies, from the inception of this nation to our present moment, are all too familiar.

The unbelievable irreverence for these lives should strike terror in us all because it amplifies a level of human cruelty that not one of us should be comfortable with accepting. If the image of the dead Black body is horrific, that horror is overshadowed by the malignant hatred that allows for the unceasing murder of Blacks. In *Titus Andronicus*, Shakespeare attends to this very horror when he interrogates the intersections of malevolence and racialized bodies. He offers his audience one of the most villainous characters in the figure of Aaron the Moor. The actions of this Black man are unequivocally heinous, but more heinous still is the unfettered racism of the white society in which he resides—that, I think, says a lot. For example, Aaron confesses to exhuming the bodies of dead men to "set them upright at their dear friends' door. / Even when their sorrows almost was forgot" (5.1.140–42).[2] On the skin of these corpses, "as on the bark of trees," Aaron carves with his knife, "Let not your sorrow die though I am dead" (5.1.138–42). As cruel and gruesome as the details of this act might be, it does not compare, in my estimation, to the utter disregard for human life that the white society exhibits to those dark of skin. Indeed, Aaron's confession to various crimes is a bargaining tool of sorts that he uses to save the life of his newborn son, the offspring of his affair with the white Queen Tamora. It is the baby's Blackness that renders him vulnerable.

What strikes me as most compelling in the case of Aaron and his baby is that there is no empathy for the life of the child beyond that which his Black father feels. When Aaron's captors hand him and his baby over to Lucius, the white nobleman chastises Aaron and disparages the baby: "here's the base fruit of that burning lust / ... / This growing image of thy fiendlike face" (5.1.43–5). Ultimately, he says of Aaron and his baby, "Hang him on this tree, / And by his side his fruit of bastardy" (5.1.46–7). Although this brutal act is never realized, Shakespeare's image of this strange hanging fruit is undeniably haunting.

Horrific acts like this, of course, have been far more than mere imaginings. That Shakespeare conceives of this strange fruit in one of his early plays—one dominated by cruelty and violated bodies—ought to signal his early understanding of the malignant reach of racism and the way his works stand to engage that reality. When Shakespeare arrives at *Othello* nearly ten years after *Titus*, he focuses explicitly on a Black character negotiating a world that devalues him because of the skin in which he lives. Through *Othello*, Shakespeare anticipates a world of interracial and intercultural exchange governed by the belief in the inferiority and dangerous potential of Blacks. In this opening chapter, then, I seek to put Shakespeare into conversation with both contemporary events and issues surrounding the violation of Black people, and with the various works, writers, and artists who address the long history of violence against Blacks. I capitalize on a call recently issued by Ian Smith, who urges us to speak of Othello so as "to see and engage from a conscious, racialized perspective (whiteness is a race too) in order to better understand race, its dependence on contested categories of difference, and the contractual complicity exercised by the dominant culture in sustaining white innocence and a strategically requisite ignorance of oppression."[3] It is not enough, Smith seems to suggest, merely to look at racism. One needs to be vividly aware of his/her/their racialized perspective when considering the systems of oppression within that play. With this in mind, this chapter urges readers to see in the brutalized bodies of Black individuals their own role and their own selves.

The necessary starting point, from where I stand, is to look deliberately at the desecrated Black body. I take my cue here from Arthur Little who, in a recent essay, admits that the news of the killing of Michael Brown—an unarmed, 18-year-old Black man shot by police in Ferguson, Missouri—was "haunting" him and impeding his ability to write.[4] "It wasn't enough," he says, "that another white cop had shot another unarmed black man (a kid really) but that the state had left his corpse in the hot streets for more than four hours."[5] Like the lynched bodies that Billie Holiday sings about in "Strange Fruit" that "rot" in the sun, Brown's lifeless body exists as an ominous reminder of the vulnerability of Black people and the acts meant to terrify and inspire fear in them. "Once again my black body was under assault," Little goes on to write about the murder of Brown.[6] With striking candor, he acknowledges the profound repercussions of repeated acts of violence upon Black men and women. Far removed from Missouri and far removed from Brown, Little felt vulnerable in his Black skin. The significance of this cannot be overstated—not for me, and not for us scholars of Shakespeare—because Arthur is our colleague, and because he is urging us to look.

Consider, then, the lifeless body of Michael Brown. On the day he was shot, the temperature in Ferguson reached 82 degrees Fahrenheit. Brown's body, face down on the street, blood flowing from a bullet hole near the eye socket and collecting into a dark pool along the hot asphalt, was left uncovered for a period of time long enough for many witnesses to take photographs and videos. The scene can only be described as grotesque. Those images were circulated in social media and on news networks. What impact, I wonder, did seeing his lifeless body have on Americans not dark of skin? What did Brown's lifeless body register for them? Hamlet's perverse description of conception—"the sun breeds maggots in a dead dog" (2.2.179)—seems particularly appropriate here, as Brown's body was treated with no more reverence than one might extend to a dead dog. But like the maggots born of a rotting carcass that Hamlet evokes, this particular image of a Black body also engenders something horrific. Surely, this young man could have been apprehended instead of being murdered. Surely, the police could have attended to his lifeless body with more urgency. Surely, his lifeless body was meant to be on display so as to send a message to the Black community in Ferguson and far beyond. Surely, many of us looked at Brown's lifeless body and have since then failed to look back. The familiarity of the violation of Black individuals and the nonexistence of justice for these murders are the horrors that Michael Brown's lifeless body engenders.

If one is Black, it would seem to be impossible to move on from this violent reality. In *Between the World and Me*, Ta-Nehisi Coates writes to his Black son, "you are the bearer of a body more fragile than any in this country. What I want you to know is that this is not your fault, even if it is ultimately your responsibility."[7] Fraught with tension, this rendering of the reality of living in Black skin in the United States—or any white majority nation, for that matter—evokes an aura of alienation, and it registers the strangeness of disembodiment that Coates so thoughtfully explores. "I believe that when they shatter the body," Coates writes, "they shatter everything … Disembodiment is a kind of terrorism, and the threat of it alters the orbit of all our lives and, like terrorism, this distortion is intentional."[8] To be Black is to be in danger of becoming the indelible "strange and bitter crop" of Billie Holiday's haunting song. This danger is evinced so profoundly in the image of Michael Brown, which is precisely what Little and Coates register through attention to their own vulnerability.

As the quintessential stranger, Shakespeare's Othello must navigate the vulnerability of his own Blackness in a white world. He endures a barrage of implicit and explicit racist comments early in the play, and he must justify his elopement with a white woman by addressing accusations that he used black magic to seduce her. When Desdemona explains that she willingly chose to be with Othello, she also says, "I saw

Othello's visage in his mind" (1.3.249).[9] While she seeks to honor Othello with this statement, she seems to suggest that she was able to locate his value somewhere beyond his physical appearance. For her audience, and perhaps for herself, she must look past his Blackness to locate his "visage" hidden somewhere within his Black body. This sentiment is reiterated when the Duke gives Brabantio these parting words of consolation: "If virtue no delighted beauty lack, / Your son-in-law is far more fair than black" (1.3.286–7).[10] To be virtuous, the Duke says, is to be white. Somehow, though, Othello has virtue in spite of his Blackness. Both Desdemona's words and the Duke's back-handed, racist compliment are uttered in the presence of Othello. We can only imagine the feeling of disembodiment that statements like this provoke.

The perception that Blackness is indicative of moral, aesthetic, and/or intellectual inferiority is one that has governed attitudes toward Blacks over time. Derrick Bell takes to task those who promote the ideas behind The Bell Curve, a book that poses flawed theories to "prove" that whites are inherently intellectually superior to Blacks. Despite universal reproof of the book among biologists, The Bell Curve enjoyed "enormous success."[11] In an attempt to makes sense of its success, Bell ultimately arrives at the conclusion that the book "captured the nation's fascination precisely because it laid out in scientific jargon what many whites believe, need desperately to believe, but dare not reveal in public or even to their private selves."[12] While the subtle racism aimed at Othello to which I allude above might register these covert feelings of white superiority, the implications of harboring such ideas are much more dire within both the play and our world. Indeed, as Bell says of The Bell Curve, it is "a perversion of truth and a provocation for racial stereotyping."[13] The results of the latter in our society often introduce life and death situations for Blacks. Of more importance, it allows so many in our nation to devalue Blacks so that their lives ultimately matter less.

Unless one is Black, one can only imagine what it must feel like to know that the skin in which you live renders your existence precarious. The reality of this should not be lost on us. In his own efforts to imagine this embodied experience, Bruce Springsteen sings of a Black mother teaching her son how to navigate interactions with police in his song "American Skin." He imagines this mother speaking to her young Black son: "She says, 'on these streets, Charles / You've got to understand the rules / If an officer stops you, promise me you'll always be polite / And that you'll never, ever run away / Promise Mama you'll keep your hands in sight.' "[14] "American Skin" was written in response to the murder of Amadou Diallo, an innocent, unarmed 22-year-old Black man who was shot 41 times by New York City police because he matched the description of a different Black man. Unfortunately, the NYPD track record regarding racial profiling, the killing of unarmed Black men and women, and systemic racism is no secret. Springsteen's song succinctly addresses our complicity in this injustice: "It ain't no secret / Ain't no secret my friend / You get killed just for living in your American skin."[15] I want to linger here because Springsteen's attention to complicity ties back to my point about Michael Brown. We know that the killings of unarmed Black men and women are unjust. We know that these killings are motivated by racism. We see their lifeless bodies scattered across our media landscape. We understand the terror. But unless one is Black, it often seems that the majority of our nation's citizens fail to feel the horror behind all of this.

When, at the closing of *Othello*, Iago has been uncovered as the catalyst for the awful crimes committed, he says to his audience, "What you know, you know" (5.2.297). To what knowledge does he allude? Peter Erickson says about these lines, "When Iago mirrors back to others their own complicity, he is faced with their obdurate refusal to know."[16] And yet, every single one of us knows. The violation of Othello's body is not one-dimensional, as it is not the work of a sole, white racist—a lone-wolf gunman, if you will. As "an extravagant and wheeling stranger / Of here and everywhere" (1.1.132–3), Othello is the consummate unknown. He is not far more fair than Black in their eyes. He is simply Black. It is difficult, then, not to wince when we see that even in literary studies, some continue to argue that the violence on Othello's body is not intrinsically connected to race. So as not to be complicit in the debasement of Black people, we evade the notion of racism and enact a double violation. We must look. "People who shut their eyes to reality," James Baldwin writes, "simply invite their own destruction, and anyone who insists on remaining in a state of innocence long after that innocence is dead turns himself into a monster."[17] And clearly, there is so much more than the "green-eyed monster" (3.3.164) at work in *Othello*. His Blackness makes monsters of them all.

Such monstrous views rooted in anti-Blackness, of course, are not limited to the actions within the play. Indeed, the manner in which audiences respond to the racism is rather telling as well. This was the case when, in August 2018, Claire Van Kampen's stage adaptation of *Othello* premiered at Shakespeare's Globe. Starring André Holland as Othello, Jessica Warbeck as Desdemona, and Mark Rylance as Iago, the play left me feeling not only underwhelmed but also perturbed by its comedic force. Critics have broached the topic of nepotism, as Rylance is married to Van Kampen, but it is fair to say that Rylance has earned a spot on that stage for other reasons. Still, his Iago came across as bumbling and even naïve. It's not that he was likeable, which would have served a certain purpose, but instead his Iago seemed a dull-witted character. It was comedy when it shouldn't have been. As Matt Wolf from the NY Times puts it, "Some productions of Othello chill the blood or, at the very least, make you ponder afresh the human capacity for psychic abrasion. But probably not until the current production at Shakespeare's Globe has this eternally bitter tragedy delivered so many laughs."[18] And herein, for me, was the true issue. The audience leaned into the laughter that Rylance provoked, and then they leaned into the racism and misogyny by laughing at it instead of expressing repulsion at the racist and sexist language. Looking up at the gifted actor, André Holland, it was difficult not to imagine that this laughter weighed heavy on him.

In an interview with NPR, Holland discussed his performance at the Globe and his early experiences with Shakespeare. He says:

> You know, when I think back to my first sort of expressing interest in Shakespeare back when I was in college—
> I'm from Alabama, and I went to college in Florida.
> And I remember the first time I sort of expressed being interested in Shakespeare. "Othello" was the first play that I was given. And at the time, I sort of took offense to it, you know? I mean, I was excited to read the play obviously, but I also thought, well, you know, why is this the only thing that's being given to me? I'd also like to play Hamlet, and I'm interested in, you know, "Coriolanus" and then all the other

plays, too. And so I rejected it for a long time. And I know a lot of other actors—you know, African-American actors have—and I assume black British actors, too—have had similar experiences. And yet, we (laughter)—we all seem to come back to it at some point, you know? But, yeah, it's a really complicated play. I mean, it's a beautifully written part, but it's not an easy one.[19]

It can't possibly be an easy one for a Black man living in a world where that kind of seemingly benign laughter must feel heinous. However vulnerable Holland might have felt, he took on the role to tell that story—and not Hamlet's. As he says later in his NPR interview, "And, you know, James Earl Jones, I think, played it six times. My friend John Douglas Thompson has played it probably four or five times, if not more. And I imagine that I probably will play it again and again, but it's going to take some time before I approach it again 'cause it is the most emotionally … draining part that I've ever played."[20] There, it seems to me, is the difference that makes some, who are more vulnerable, capable of recognizing the heavy nature of Shakespeare and race, then and now.

It should come as no surprise, then, that for many scholars and actors of color, *Othello* is not only an incredibly difficult play to digest but also one that they are not interested in entertaining. Ayanna Thompson, for example, says of the play in an interview:

I hate this play. [Laughter]. I hate the audience members when they laugh. I hate the actors who are, you know, kind of seem to be enjoying saying these vile, racist slurs. I hate the fact that those poor black actors have to endure it night after night after night. In some ways, to me, it feels like a toxic play. At some point I'm like, why are we returning to these plays? [Laughter] Why aren't we doing productions where you can see black rage articulated in a way that is, like, "I'm better than you," as opposed to a production where the black man constantly is like, "Oh my God, my secret fear is that I'm not as good as you." You know, I end up consulting with a lot of classical actors, and I end up being brought in to productions where black actors are feeling very vulnerable when they're playing Othello, and if the theater company isn't set up in such a way where that actor feels emotionally supported, it can be a traumatic event—and [laughter], like, I don't think in the same way that it is for actors who play King Lear. It's a different kind of trauma that we're asking those actors to go through.[21]

Thompson's thoughtful take on this reality for Black actors is vital to understanding the stakes behind staging *Othello* in our day. The above reference to Holland ought to illustrate precisely the type of trauma to which Thompson alludes. Just as important, though, from my estimation, is Thompson's attention to the way the play makes *her* feel as an audience member.

Ayanna and I attended Van Kampen's Globe production together, and we found ourselves exchanging glances in disbelief again and again as the laughter surrounded us. It was, to say the least, emotionally difficult to see and hear so many people in that predominantly white audience laugh along with the racism. But isn't that precisely what is transpiring in our current moment as the U.S. President provides fodder for white supremacists and closet racists alike to feed on the vulnerability of Black and brown individuals? Nothing about that laughter was benign. Nothing about the racism at the highest level of our democracy is benign. It is malignancy on par with the evil that Iago exhibits.

In his own exploration of this malignancy, Baldwin considers the branding of Blacks with moral darkness that allows for whites to justify the terror that they feel. It is a terror, he writes, "which activates a lynch mob"—akin to that which prompted the burning of would-be witches.[22] He goes on:

> One need not, indeed, search for examples so historic or gaudy; this is a warfare waged daily in the heart, a warfare so vast, so relentless and so powerful that the interracial handshake or the interracial marriage can be as crucifying as the public hanging or the secret rape. This panic motivates our cruelty, this fear of the dark makes it impossible that our lives shall be other than superficial; this, interlocked with and feeding our glittering, mechanical, inescapable civilization which has put to death our freedom.[23]

As in the case that I mention above where we cannot look away from the bodies of the Black men and women who are unjustly murdered, we cannot look away from this reality either. It is present and it is here in our very moment. Baldwin's admission, "I had discovered the weight of white people in the world,"[24] is remarkably relevant as we look out at a society that devalues Blacks—a society where the belief by many, and by many in positions of power, that Black lives matter less is not reason enough, it seems, to compel a sizeable portion of our population to call for widespread reform or revolution. That, too, reveals a particular malignancy.

When we look to Shakespeare's *Othello*, then, we don't witness the kind of confidence that Thompson wishes we would see. It's simply not there. The Black rage that Othello displays is the rage that many non-Black individuals expect from Black men and women alike. It is a justifiable rage, and one that should be expressed. In his stunning play, *American Moor*, Keith Hamilton Cobb considers the parameters of tapping into this type of rage for Black actors playing Othello. *American Moor* imagines a Black actor named Keith auditioning for the role of Othello while confronting, quite explicitly, the racism that surrounds such auditions. The actor says of his early encounters with Shakespeare's works: "You know, it was never written to be read. It was written to be seen, and heard. And the moment I realized that, I realized that the only thing lacking from what I had been reading was me."[25] He contends with this invisibility—with his invisibility—by interrogating, quite masterfully, the white structures that allow for his erasure.

In ways that most readers of Shakespeare might not necessarily be able to understand, Cobb outlines the apprehensions surrounding a Black actor undertaking a role about a Black man imagined by a white man for a white audience. For so very long, Othello's value was and continues to be delineated by white readers and directors. Within this powerful play, Cobb addresses these oppressive structures when he interacts with the voice of a white director and speaks aloud what he wishes he could say to him. For example, the Director explains to the Black actor Othello's motivations when he is brought before the senate: "And he really needs to charm this senate with this gift of oratory and tale-weaving that he has in order to prevail. So, let me see him ingratiate himself a little more to them, I mean, the senate thrives on … uh … obeisance … Right?" To this, the Actor first tells himself, "Put on your poker face, Brotha," and then wonders if he sees the "faintest of smiles" on the Director's face.[26] He then launches into this imagined response to the Director:

> You think that he thinks that he needs to do … "a number" for these guys, in order to succeed in getting from them the thing that *you* think he wants … And so, in order to get this gig, ah no wait! … in order to succeed in getting from *you* the thing that *you* think *I* want … you're implying that *I* need to do "a number …" for *you* … It's brilliant. You're sittin' there lookin' expectantly at me, thinkin' we're speaking the same language. But you wouldn't understand a single word of all that's *not* being said … if I said it … if Othello said it … Gotdammit … I know that your intentions are good, young man, and that this is not your fault … My anger, Othello's anger, the guard dog, forever snarling at his chain's end, sooner to strangle himself than acquiesce to your energy, he does not see you. He sees all the hovering forces in this room, in that senate chamber, in the world that have *made* you you, as they are all the same forces that have never allowed me to be me. I'm sorry … You stand in for so much, but I do too, and I cannot just be me, for you are never, ever, only you.
>
> **Breathe**, Negro! … You're an actor. You're supposed to be open, available to this "creative process …" But, you see, in matters of race, throughout my American life, whenever some white person, well-meaning or otherwise, has asked me to "be open" they have invariably meant, "See it my way." And in this instance, in *this* play, that is unacceptable. You think I want to be **your** Othello. And, God bless you, you have every right to think that. But it's your first mistake. And you're not alone.[27]

In the "hovering forces" that Cobb imagines, I cannot help but recognize the weight of whiteness to which Baldwin alludes. With brilliant strength, Cobb captures here the kind of confident Black rage that Thompson wishes she would see in productions of *Othello*. It is the kind of rage that an actor needs to bring to *Othello*. As the Actor suggests, he is "never allowed" to be himself even as the white Director is "never, ever" only himself—but rather, a representation of myopic whiteness. That fact, the actor says, is "unacceptable" where rendering Othello is concerned. That a white man thinks he can understand and unpack how a Black man feels when addressing a white audience is, indeed, an egregious error. And it is an error that so many readers and directors of Shakespeare make.

It is here, in Cobb's keen attention to the shades of racism that so often centralize whiteness and ignore, if not silence, those dark of skin, that I see him carry Shakespeare into a meaningful realm in our present moment. He carries *Othello* beyond productions that perpetuate racist views. We need to see such rage that calls out those who continue to weaponize Shakespeare to undergird structures of white supremacy. We need to speak of Othello (as Smith urges us to do), see the violated Black body (as Little urges us to do), and recognize the consistent attempts to displace Black confidence (as Cobb urges us to do) if we want to understand why Shakespeare matters in our day. We need to see Shakespeare from perspectives that, quite often, do not matter as much to audiences accustomed to seeing the play through the eyes of whiteness.

It should come as little surprise, then, that one of the most important writers of our generation—who thoughtfully interrogates how most readers have been "positioned as white"[28]—imagined the possibilities behind giving a silenced Black woman in *Othello* a voice to speak back. In her play *Desdemona*, Toni Morrison creates an afterworld where the various characters both within and imagined through *Othello* interact. As its director, Peter Sellars, explains, though, the key idea for the play grew out of Desdemona's reference to her mother's maid, Barbary. This reference to "another African character in his play," Sellars argues, "triggers surprising associations."[29] Not the least significant of these associations was the fact that Barbary was more than likely Desdemona's mother's slave and not her "maid."

When Desdemona ultimately sees Barbary, her excitement is palpable. "Barbary! Barbary. Come closer," Desdemona says.[30] She goes on: "How I have missed you. Remember the days we spent by the canal? We ate sweets and you saved the honey for me eating none yourself. We shared so much."[31] Desdemona's memories of Barbary are clearly tender, and these memories include the perceived kindness of Barbary. However, Barbary has memories of her own, and her response is quite telling. Barbary offers this response to Desdemona, "We shared nothing."[32] The disparity between what Desdemona and Barbary remember is critical in understanding the power structures between a white and a Black woman. It also recalls the type of acquiescence to which Cobb so profoundly alludes in his own play.

Barbary must give to Desdemona, and thus it is true that nothing is shared. It is the privilege of whiteness and her high social standing that allow Desdemona to imagine she shared something with Barbary in the asymmetrical relationship. As the conversation unfolds, we learn that Barbary is actually a slave named Sa'ran:

Desdemona: What do you mean?
Sa'ran: I mean you don't even know my name. Barbary? Barbary
　　　　　is what you call Africa. Barbary is the geography of the

foreigner, the savage. Barbary? Barbary equals the sly, vicious enemy who must be put down at any price; held down at any cost for the conquerors' pleasure. Barbary is the name of those without whom you could neither live nor prosper.

Desdemona: So tell me. What is your name?

Sa'ran: Sa'ran.

Desdemona: Well, Sa'ran, whatever your name, you were my best friend.

Sa'ran: I was your slave.

Desdemona: What does that matter? I have known and loved you all my life.

Sa'ran: I am black-skinned. You are white-skinned.[33]

Here, Sa'ran ultimately arrives at the structures of power relations that uphold white supremacy. She casts light on the racist views of Africans and when she identifies herself by name, Desdemona's response makes manifest the snide attitudes towards those darker of skin—"Well, Sa'ran, whatever your name." The idea here, of course, is that Sa'ran's view of herself matters less to Desdemona than the version of reality Desdemona has constructed. In both Desdemona's mind in Morrison's play and in the mind of the white director of *American Moor*, the Black individual's disposition and motivations are thought to be better understood by somebody who is white.

The problem with this, of course, is that it is not just a matter of foreclosing on the Black perspective—of ignoring the Black experience—but rather it is indicative of structures where such privileging of whiteness opens the door for the atrocities that have transpired across our nation's temporal and geographical landscape. It is indicative of the horrific history of strange fruit that this nation has witnessed. The seemingly benign acts of whites "knowing better" or the willful ignoring of unjust power structures are, in so many ways, the very backbone of white supremacy. It is a complicity as grotesque as the violent acts meant to make visible such "supremacy." And while it is certainly important to look at the desecrated Black body on which such acts occur, as I have done above, it is equally important to look squarely at those who are capable of such desecration.

The truth is, it isn't really one's dark skin that renders one expendable. When considering how Americans look—with a play on "look" as both noun and verb—Karen Fields and Barbara Fields write:

> Deference rules, variable sumptuary codes, mistaken shootings by police, and border monitoring of segregated spaces all stand in reference to a person as a seen "object." That reference entails, besides, a seeing object and of course a seeing subject. These varied sightlines of racecraft are not separate phenomena. They occur together or in rapid sequence, and in constantly shifting perspectives.[34]

We should look closely, then, at the seeing subject when it comes to the strange fruit to which I alluded at the opening of this chapter. In her interrogation surrounding white rage, Carol Anderson meticulously outlines the unflagging efforts to keep Black Americans disempowered throughout the history of the United States. In the process, Anderson allows her readers a glimpse of the truly heinous acts by those who epitomize the monstrosity behind white rage. She relates the story of Mary Turner, who in 1918 was rightfully angry and protesting the lynching of her husband, who had zero connection to a crime committed by a different Black man—a man who had already been lynched for killing an abusive white man named Hampton Smith. I quote Anderson at length here, because I want to be sure we think about the seeing subject—that we see what these men, who vehemently clung to their whiteness, saw when they lynched Turner:

> They dragged Mary to a tree, stripped her, tied her ankles together and strung her upside down. The men ran to their cars, brought back gasoline, and began "to roast her alive." Then they saw her naked, eight-month-pregnant stomach convulsing. That only set the mob, made up of several Hampton Smith's brothers, as well as a clerk in the post office, an auditor for Standard Oil, a furniture salesman, and several farmers, into a deeper frenzy, as one man took out his knife and sliced away at her charred flesh until the baby ripped out of the womb, fell to the ground and gave two cries. Someone in the lynch party then stepped forward and smashed the child's head into the red Georgia dirt with the heel of his boot.[35]

This dreadful act, Anderson reminds us, was not unique in, or to, the South. Such vicious violence on men and women dark of skin is not unique. Its temporal and geographic ubiquity is firmly in place, and we should all be confronting this monstrosity head on. And we know that these violent acts are not something uncomfortably nestled in our nation's past. This pervasive, violent racism cuts across geographical and temporal spaces and it calls attention to the widespread complicity. Indeed, Fields and Fields describe the everyday nature of the occupations these vicious men held—farmers, a furniture salesman, a post office clerk, and an auditor for Standard Oil.

Henry Clay Folger, founder of the Folger Shakespeare library, was the president of Standard Oil at the time this auditor partook in that heinous murder. In no way do I mean to implicate Folger in this horrific act, but I do want to draw attention to the seeming ordinariness and proximity of individuals capable of cutting out a baby from a murdered mother's womb and crushing it with their heel. It is a malevolence that knows no bounds. One wonders how men like that return home to their families, their children, their jobs.

I think, then, about the desire of the white men in *Titus Andronicus* to hang Aaron and "his fruit of bastardy"—his newborn son—beside him. Shakespeare's plays alert us to this desire for violence—to the various forms of white rage. After all, the office clerks, furniture salesmen, farmers, and, yes, college professors who are capable of such vicious, racist violence are all around us. Although I appreciate efforts to see in Shakespeare's works some real sense of hope in uncovering the calls for compassionate and humane treatment of others, in this moment, from our present perspective, I feel it might serve us better if we—as scholars, educators, students, and readers who engage Shakespeare—look to the racist moments that reveal to us and allow us to consider thoughtfully the weight of whiteness and the grotesque nature of white supremacy.

NOTES

1 Billie Holiday, "Strange Fruit" (1939). Lyrics written by Abel Meeropol.
2 William Shakespeare, *Titus Andronicus*, ed. Barbara Mowat and Paul Werstine. (New York: Folger Shakespeare Library, 2005).
3 Ian Smith, "We are Othello: Speaking of Race in Early Modern Studies," *Shakespeare Quarterly* 67.1 (2016), 122.
4 Arthur Little, "Re-Historicizing Race, White Melancholia, and the Shakespeare Property," *Shakespeare Quarterly* 67.1 (2016), 84–5.

5   Ibid., 85.

6   Ibid., 85.

7   Ta-Nehisi Coates, *Between the World and Me* (New York: Spiegel and Grau, 2015), 137.

8   Ibid., 113–24.

9   For the use of these lines as a springboard for a thoughtful discussion of color-coded discourse in the play as it relates to the concurrent perpetuation and disruption of the process of empire, see Ambereen Dadabhoy, "Two Faced: The Problem of Othello's Visage," *Othello: State of Play*, ed. Lena Cowen Orlin (London: Arden, 2014), 121–48.

10 For a keen reading of these lines and the implications behind them, see Peter Erickson, "Race Words in *Othello*," *Shakespeare and Immigration*, ed. Ruben Espinosa and David Ruiter (Burlington, VT: Ashgate, 2014), 159–76.

11 Derrick Bell, "Who's Afraid of Critical Race Theory?," *University of Illinois Law Review* 4 (1995), 894.

12 Ibid., 898.

13 Ibid., 898.

14 Bruce Springsteen, "American Skin," *Live in New York City* (2001).

15 Michael Cooper, "Officers in Bronx Fire 41 Shots, And an Unarmed Man Is Killed," *New York Times*, February 5, 1999, www.nytimes.com/1999/02/05/nyregion/officers-in-bronx-fire-41-shots-and-an-unarmed-man-is-killed.html

16 Erickson, "Race Words," 170.

17 James Baldwin, *Notes of a Native Son* (Boston, MA: Beacon Press, 1955), 178.

18 Matt Wolf, "Laughs from 'Othello,' and a Swoon From 'Little Shop of Horrors,'" *New York Times*, August 30, 2018.

19 Terry Gross, "André Holland Explores: 'Where I Fit, How I Fit, If I Fit,'" NPR, August 22, 2018. www.npr.org/templates/transcript/transcript.php?storyId=640876704

20 Ibid.

21 Isaac Butler, "Othello," *Lend Me Your Ears: A Podcast About Shakespeare and Modern Politics*, Podcast audio, September 11, 2018. https://podcasts.apple.com/us/podcast/5-othello/id1382357065?i=1000419521754

22 Baldwin, *Notes of a Native Son*, 18.

23 Ibid., 18.

24 Ibid., 90.

25 Keith Hamilton Cobb, *American Moor* (London: Methuen, 2020), 4. I would like to extend my gratitude to Keith Hamilton Cobb for his willingness to share a copy of his then unpublished script with me early in the process of writing this book. The original script is housed at the Folger Shakespeare Library.

26 Ibid., 16–17.

27 Ibid., 17–18.

28 Toni Morrison, *Playing in the Dark: Whiteness and the Literary Imagination* (New York: Vintage Books, 1992), xii.

29 Peter Sellars, "Forward," *Desdemona*, Toni Morrison (London: Oberon Books, 2012), 8.

30 Toni Morrison, *Desdemona* (London: Oberon Books, 2012), 45.

31 Ibid., 45.

32 Ibid., 45.

33 Ibid., 45.

34 Karen Fields and Barbara Fields, *Racecraft: The Soul of Inequality in American Life* (London: Verso, 2012), 70.

35 Ibid., 40.

Two

Luis Alberto Urrea's *The Devil's Highway* traces the tragic experiences of "the Yuma 14"—14 Mexican men who traveled through treacherous desert terrain in hopes of entering into the United States, but most of whom did not survive that journey.[1] In the afterword to his powerful book, Urrea explains that despite the completion of that project, the stories surrounding issues of immigration "never stop coming":

> Item: Hope College, a Christian school in Holland, Michigan, sponsored an immigration week. They had every student wear a T-shirt that read: WWJD? Under it, not the usual *What Would Jesus Do?* But the more provocative: *Who Would Jesus Deport?*

> Item: in the desert, I saw a border enforcement Minuteman wearing a What Would Jesus Do? rubber bracelet. The same day, I saw a liberal Presbyterian activist putting out water bottles for the immigrants with a What Would Jesus Do? rubber bracelet. I thought: Shotguns or water?[2]

The question, of course, is absurd. Or at least it should be. Water. At every turn, the answer is water. Urrea's focal point, however, is the shared religious affinities between those carrying weapons, in an unofficial capacity, both to patrol the

U.S. Mexico border and to intimidate and threaten individuals seeking refuge in the United States and those who see in those immigrants lives worth saving. To ask, what, in that scenario, Jesus would do is to consider what a Christian following in the path and teachings of Christ should do. That these two individuals arrive at such different answers demonstrates how divergent ideas of Christianity in this country have become. Perhaps a different way to phrase it for these two individuals is: What Would Your Jesus Do?

The pressing need to validate one's humane acts through the authority of a Christian framework speaks to the fraught nature of immigration in our day. The moral imperative to consider a compassionate understanding when it comes to those seeking refuge is, it seems, not enough. One has to signal to one's audience that these acts of kindness (or, for the Minuteman, acts of terror) are justifiable because in these moments one follows in the path of Jesus. For me, it calls to mind a YouTube video I came across when researching that archive for my work on Shakespeare and immigration. The video, "William Shakespeare would support the Commissioners' ICE Resolution,"[3] immediately caught my attention because, in some ways, it posed a question similar to that on the rubber bracelets: What Would William Shakespeare Do?

In this 2009 video, Joseph Madden, a Chatham County resident and Franciscan friar, addresses the Chatham County Board of Commissioners in Pittsboro, North Carolina and voices his support for a proposed resolution that would oppose "any local agency contracting with the U.S. Immigration and Customs Enforcement (ICE) for the purpose of enforcing federal immigration laws."[4] The idea was to avoid adopting something akin to Arizona's own Senate Bill 1070, which was designed to "discourage and deter the unlawful entry and presence of aliens and economic activity by persons unlawfully present in the United States" by granting local law enforcement permission to arrest suspected undocumented immigrants.[5] Arizona's SB 1070 led to widespread racial profiling and, quite frankly, afforded local law enforcement officials to act on their racist tendencies.

For Madden, it seems, the threat of allowing local law enforcement agencies to harass the immigrant community in North Carolina led him to speak up on their behalf. In his opening argument, Madden says, "I would like to quote from the great Shakespeare who speaks through Shylock." Somewhat predictably, Madden quotes Shylock's "Hath not a Jew eyes?" speech to emphasize Shakespeare's own "humanitarian" stance:

> I am a Jew. Hath not a Jew eyes? Hath not a Jew hands, organs, dimensions, senses, affections, passions? Fed with the same food, hurt with the same weapons, subject to the same diseases, healed by the same means, warmed and cooled by the same winter and summer as a Christian is? If you prick us, do we not bleed? If you tickle us, do we not laugh? If you poison us, do we not die?
>
> (3.1.57–65)[6]

Madden says of Shakespeare, "I suggest he speaks for all immigrants. Now that's if you would substitute immigrants for Jews."[7] He then offers a "theological" argument to explain how "on the sixth day" God created man in his own image, and this—of course—included undocumented immigrants. The glaring omission of Shylock's forced conversion and egregious oppression aside, Madden's intent is to employ

Shakespeare to argue for inclusion. What is striking to me, however, is the fact that he deploys Shakespeare's social capital before drawing on God's currency. Shakespeare's authority informs his humanitarian argument. That Shakespeare favors immigrants is hardly a given, but that his cultural ubiquity matters certainly is.

Behind Shakespeare's works, readers like Madden sympathetic to those oppressed and marginalized often seek to locate an ethics of hospitality. Take, for example, the short film produced by the International Rescue Committee and Shakespeare's Globe, "The Strangers' Case—Shakespeare's Rallying Cry for Humanity."[8] In this production, refugees from Syria, Sierra Leone, and South Sudan recite a speech from Sir Thomas More, one thought to be written by Shakespeare. Images of refugee camps are interspliced with the actors reciting More's speech, and visually, this is clearly meant to inspire sympathy and pity for those watching the film. The passage, spoken by More in an attempt to suppress an English mob intent on enacting violence on immigrants in London, appeals to a humane understanding of the plight of immigrants. I quote here the lengthy portion of the speech that the actors recite:

> Imagine that you see the wretched strangers,
> Their babies at their backs, with their poor luggage,
> Plodding to th' ports and coasts for transportation,
> And that you sit as kings in your desires,
> Authority quite silenced by your brawl,
> And you in ruff of your opinions clothed:
> What had you got? I'll tell you: you had taught
> How insolence and strong hand should prevail,
> How order should be quelled. And by this pattern

Not one of you should live an aged man;
For other ruffians, as their fancies wrought,
With selfsame hand, self reasons, and self right,
Would shark on you, and men, like ravenous fishes,
Would feed on one another.
[...]
[...] Say now the King,
[...]
Should so much come too short of your great trespass
As to but banish you: whither would you go?
What country, by the nature of your error,
Should give you harbor? Go you to France or Flanders,
To any German province, Spain or Portugal,
Nay, anywhere that not adheres to England:
Why, you must needs be strangers. Would you be pleased
To find a nation of such barbarous temper
That, breaking out in hideous violence,
Would not afford you an abode on earth,
Whet their detested knives against your throats,
Spurn you like dogs, and like as if that God
Owed not nor made not you, nor that the elements
Were not appropriate to your comforts
But chartered unto them? What would you think
To be thus used? This is the strangers' case,
And this your mountainish inhumanity.

(6.83–156)[9]

As the actors in the short film close out their speech with these lines, the words on the screen read, "This is Shakespeare's rallying cry for humanity. Now it's your turn."[10] One can recognize in More's speech something similar to the option posed by Urrea—shotgun or water? The film, literally recited center stage at Shakespeare's Globe, encourages us to consider: What would Shakespeare do? What will you do?

I find no fault in Madden or those behind the International Rescue Committee and Shakespeare's Globe collaboration for locating in Shakespeare's works moments that call for compassionate treatment of others. In both Shylock's and More's speeches, we see an appeal for their audience to put themselves in the shoes of immigrants, foreigners, and strangers. In practice, though, this is no easy feat. In practice, civilian men patrol the border wearing "WWJD" rubber bracelets while holding a rifle in their arms ready to take aim at exhausted human beings seeking a better life. Indeed, the animosity against not only Sudanese, Syrian, and Latin American refugees but also many others attempting to escape brutal violence by seeking refuge is widespread. This kind of xenophobia also surrounds Shylock and the immigrants of *Sir Thomas More*. Rather than tender another reading of Shakespeare's works that allows us to imagine what Shakespeare would do in an effort to imagine a humane understanding of others, though, I instead want to consider how his works demonstrate to us the callousness of a racist society. I, too, want to draw on Shakespeare's social capital, but I want to do so by confronting the ugly racism both within and without his works. In this way, we will not have to pretend to know what Shakespeare would do, but rather we can consider what *we* need to do in the face of such vile injustice.

Shotguns or water? If we can consider what it means to be in want of water, we can perhaps begin to recognize the horrific policies and practices that deny dignity to so many who make their way to the U.S. Mexico borderlands. As I mention above, the practices stem beyond our militarized border, as civilians have taken it upon themselves to hunt for immigrants. For those attempting to offer humanitarian aid to migrants crossing the desert in/near Arizona, the threat of arrest and prosecution is very real. Indeed, U.S. Government authorities have kicked over and slashed water jugs left for migrants along the desert, and they are aggressively prosecuting volunteers who seek to help migrants—with fines of up to $10,000.[11] Such acts are meant to signal an unequivocal refusal, at any level, to aid migrants seeking to enter the United States. The message of inhospitality is solidly in place. As in the case with Michael Brown that I explored in the previous chapter, such profound irreverence for human life breeds something monstrous. To disregard the suffering that so many immigrants encounter on their journeys to the U.S. Mexico border is to validate the idea that brown lives—like Black lives—matter less. On a fundamental level, we must acknowledge that what these migrants want is to survive. That the kind act of leaving water so as to prevent death from dehydration or heat stroke is foreclosed upon by our government officials is testament to the fact that we are so far from being an exceptional nation.

In her stunning title poem from her collection, *For Want of Water*, Sasha Pimentel draws on the true story of a migrant mother who died of dehydration as she crossed into the United States with her son.[12] Like many immigrants, this mother was seeking a better life for her child, and Pimentel poignantly captures the thirst to begin a life anew against the reality that, in such searching, the water sometimes does not come. The poem opens:

An ant will drown himself, his body submerging
   into ease, his mandibles, head, antennae, baptized. How lovely

to lose your senses to the cup of your want. A boy
    drags his mother's body across the desert, her fluids rising
        to heaven in order to quench her skin. How divine
            her body must have looked, clutched at the ankles, her
arms reaching out in exultation, her head stippled in rings
  of sand and blood as he walked with her, slowly, her fallen
      and moving shape the fork of a divining rod, her body shaking
          with each of his steps, and for water, shaking to find
              that deep and secret tributary ...[13]

The yearning that Pimentel evokes is palpable, and this woman in search of water instead finds death. What Pimentel works through in her poem is the underlying beauty of such searching while articulating, with candid clarity, the physical fracturing that transpires during journeys like that of this mother and her son. In that mother's dying body, Pimentel locates the full weight of migration, thirst, and most importantly for this present study, the inhospitable treatment of those rendered illegitimate.

It isn't just a matter of humanizing those migrants encountering brutal inhospitality—it is a matter of understanding the devastating effects of such inhospitality. It is a matter of casting light on those individuals and entities who choose to dehumanize immigrants. Pimentel points out that "this is a common story," and that "the boy / is not a boy now but every boy we have ever known."[14] When the other migrants help the boy lift his mother and make it to a mall parking lot on the U.S. side of the border, people "from behind windows" call the police, who arrive "with their handcuffs and call her *dead*."[15] The boy refuses to hear this. Pimentel continues:

... To call would be to remember all
the other times that he has called for her, and the boy plugs his
ears, shakes his head, doesn't know that he cannot physically
produce tears anymore—such thirst can rid us of these
symbols—
only that now there are mouths around him calling
other names
as men run and other men give chase, because how much do
you need
to give up in order to stay? a boy? a mother? your land and inner
land? ...[16]

In her unflinching attention to this incident, Pimentel locates the thirst and heartbreak of a boy who has done nothing wrong, and yet who finds himself apprehended and in want of water, a mother, and a motherland. It is difficult, then, not to see in this the loss of one's homeland and also the loss of the land of imagined belonging that never allows one to belong. That signals the evaporation of the American dream. What we see is mistrust and a militarized border where immigrants are made to feel that any sense of belonging will forever be out of reach. Such is the plight of those brown of skin attempting to make their way to the United States. In our current political landscape, this is applicable to many Latinxs who have known the United States as their only home and yet are made to feel like outsiders here. Often it feels like there is no legitimacy for Latinxs in the United States. Somebody always seems to be waiting from behind a window to make you feel lesser than.

What, then, can such alienation, inhospitality, and perceived illegitimacy teach us about Shakespeare? Again, I'm not invested here in trying to explain what Shakespeare would do, but rather I want to think through how we can use his plays to think about such struggle. What can we bring to his plays when it comes to interrogating one's access to a stable feeling of belonging? Perhaps no play engages the topic of legitimacy more straightforwardly than *King Lear*. When Gloucester's illegitimate son, Edmund, contemplates his status, he blames the "plague of custom" and the "curiosity of nations" for defining his status as a "bastard" (1.2.3–4).[17] While we can easily recognize in "the plague of custom" his attention to social conventions, the second comment about the "curiosity of nations" inherently gestures at difference. On the one hand, Edmund obviously seems to refer to legal divisions about status defined by the state. But the term "nation" also calls to mind the grouping of individuals by cultural, linguistic, religious, and/ or geographic commonalities. One of many examples of this comes from Shylock in *The Merchant of Venice* when he says of the Christian merchant Antonio: "He hates our sacred nation" (1.3.48).[18] Here Shylock makes reference to the Jewish community. In a similar vein, when in *Henry V* the Welsh Fluellen says to the Irish MacMorris, "there is not many of your nation," MacMorris responds, "Of my nation? What ish my nation?" (3.2.121–25).[19] Here, the play deploys both MacMorris' Irish accent and Fluellen's inexact command of English to highlight the differences between their respective "nations" and that of the English, even as they have come together to fight with the English against the French. I will return to *Henry V* later in this chapter, but here I want to highlight how Edmund's passing comment in *King Lear* is loaded because the seeming "curiosity of nations" suggests something strange behind the very act of delineating difference. On some level, we can all recognize the arbitrary nature of the way so many communities are imagined, especially where perceptions of national belonging are concerned, but it is Edmund's keen use of "curiosity" that piques my interest.[20]

As he contemplates his own situation, Edmund arrives at the conclusion that it is simply a matter of the circumstances surrounding his birth that defines his illegitimacy. It seems so incredibly arbitrary, and yet this arbitrary delineation will define these individuals to others for the rest of his life. Edmund says,

> ... Why "bastard"? wherefore "base,"
> When my dimensions are as well compact,
> My mind as generous and my shape as true,
> As honest madam's issue? Why brand they us
> With "base," with "baseness," "bastardy," "base," "base,"
> Who, in the lusty stealth of nature, take
> More composition and fierce quality
> Than doth within a dull, stale, tired bed
> Go to th' creating a whole tribe of fops
> Got 'tween sleep and wake? Well then,
> Legitimate Edgar, I must have your land.
> Our father's love is to the bastard Edmund
> As to th' legitimate, Fine word, "legitimate."
> Well, my legitimate, if this letter speed,
> And my invention thrive, Edmund the base
> Shall top the legitimate. I grow, I prosper.
> Now, gods, stand up for bastards!

(1.2.1–23)

Edmund straightforwardly takes on the topic of illegitimacy, but he also attends to the notion of passion when it comes to one's constitution. At the onset, Edmund juxtaposes what is natural against societal customs that deem individuals born out of wedlock as inferior. "Why bastard ... where-fore base?" he asks. Those branded with "baseness" and "bastardy," he says, are in fact of "fiercer quality" because they were conceived in the "lusty stealth of nature." Those deemed "legitimate," on the other hand, were conceived in the lethargy of a "dull, stale, tired bed." Although Edmund makes illegitimacy sound outright exciting, it is the ambition behind his words that charges this contemplation of legitimacy with such force. For the better part of the play, he thrives. He navigates the political situation with dexterity, and he finds himself on the verge of becoming the King of England. But what are the implications of this ambition from this side of our historical divide.

When we consider how Edmund's attention to ambition might register for audiences when spoken by actors of color as opposed to white actors in our present moment, we might recognize how the significance of terms like "base" and "legitimate" infuses contemporary understandings of Shakespeare's purchase with a "fiercer quality." Ambition, when linked to Black and brown individuals, carries distinct possibilities and, indeed, very real precariousness, because it stands to provoke what Carol Anderson calls "white rage." As Anderson notes, "The trigger for white rage, inevitably, is black advancement. It is not the mere presence of black people that is the problem; rather, it is blackness with ambition, with drive, with purpose, with aspirations, and with demand for full and equal citizenship."[21] How this rage manifests, then, is of critical importance. While we might imagine a mob of white supremacists attacking people of color when we think of white rage, we should recognize that it does not need to be so explicitly violent to have truly horrific consequences. Anderson argues:

White rage is not about visible violence, but rather it works its way through the courts, the legislatures, and a range of government bureaucracies. It wreaks havoc subtly, almost imperceptibly. Too imperceptibly, certainly, for a nation consistently drawn to the spectacular—to what it can see. It's not the Klan. White rage doesn't have to wear sheets, burn crosses, or take to the streets. Working the halls of power, it can achieve its ends far more effectively, fare more destructively.[22]

To be clear, Anderson here is exploring white rage in connection to the Black experience. However, as I mention in my introduction, I want to locate entry points to scrutinize shared experiences of expendability for Black and brown people. When we consider how Edmund's words, when spoken by an actor of color or—perhaps more prevalently— when understood through the lens of readers who are Black or brown, we recognize that his ambition takes on the ener- gies of resistance. However, I won't linger on that optimistic- ally driven perspective of resistance too long, as it is indeed the "curiosity of nations" that encapsulates the nefarious nature of keeping some "illegitimate" individuals subjugated. It is the object of resistance that we ought to scrutinize.

Recognizing a similar "curiosity" in our own day allows us to look, head on, at systems of oppression that perpetuate racial inequities and reveal to us the shades of racism in our nation. What is at stake when Black advancement is a real possibility? What is at stake when the idea of equal citizen- ship for those darker of skin becomes a reality? What does it matter when Black voter turnout is above average on any given election year? Why does the idea of equal citizenship between whites and those darker of skin strike terror, anger, resentment, and hatred in so many? The curiosity of nations in our day imagines those darker of skin as perpetual outsiders. And make no mistake about it, our government reacts to such ambition. Voter suppression is real, and it always targets Black and brown communities. Those who believe that Black and brown people are born base also believe that it is their obligation to keep us there.

Edmund's underscoring of "base" and "baseness" signals to his audience that this is where his own value as a human being has been positioned simply because he was born out of wedlock. And yet *King Lear* invites us to focus on Edmund's villainy. If his soliloquy provokes any sense of sympathy and ostensible support for his design where the "base" is able to top the "legitimate," his evil actions overshadow the maliciousness behind the structures that define him from the very beginning. We need to interrogate those structures—a dishonest, unjust father and a social hierarchy that ignores those "poor naked wretches" with "houseless heads and unfed sides" while espousing perceptions of nobility and worth based on birthrights (3.4.33–4). Because one is born into certain conditions, one is imagined to be superior or, conversely, inferior. The same, of course, can be argued about being born white within a society that values whiteness above all else. When it comes to racism, these structures endure. When Black and brown individuals seek to call out injustices, any kind of ambition akin to Edmund's own—ambition that threatens to disrupt such structures—is often met with a distinct white rage. In the dark skin I'm in, some individuals see *me* as a threat to their existence.

It isn't really our dark skin that renders us expendable, but instead it is those who glare at us because of our dark skin that are the actual threat. Deep seated racism much too often leads to the murder of innocent people because of the skin they're in. Indeed, this recently happened in my own hometown of El Paso, Texas. Patrick Crusius, a 21-year-old white terrorist, drove 600 miles from Dallas to the border city of El Paso with the explicit intent of killing, in his words, "as many Mexicans as he could."[23] He drove into a busy Walmart parking lot off Interstate-10. He first walked into Walmart unarmed, law enforcement officials explained, to survey the store and "size up" the clientele where there were approximately 1,000–3,000 customers—men, women, children of all ages shopping on an otherwise ordinary Saturday morning. School would begin soon that month, and many were there gathering supplies to begin the school year. Little did they know that they were being stalked like animals. Satisfied with what he saw, Crusius went back to his vehicle to prepare. He put on protective earmuffs, so as not to damage his hearing. He put on safety glasses to protect his eyes. He was a fully armed hunter wearing his racism on his sleeve. Before even stepping foot into the store, he began firing his AK-47 indiscriminately. People scattered in fear, but so very many were unable to escape that brutal violence. When the horrific massacre came to an end, 22 people were dead.

Seriously, though, what else should we expect? Prior to this awful event, children were already being separated from their parents and families at the border, and our government was caging brown people like animals. Those acts committed by our own government—along with the unending acts of police brutality against Black men and women again, and again, and again—do not exist in some vacuum. Those acts signal to others that this is the way they, too, should see Black and brown people. Of course that white man felt emboldened and entitled to act like a would-be hunter traversing his state—his nation, what he feels *belongs* to him—and to come into this city that has never been his own in an effort to kill those whose brown skin threatened his property and his whiteness.[24] It is the insidious workings of white rage that reify narratives dehumanizing those darker of skin and rendering our existence precarious.

How, in the face of such racial injustice, do we approach a play like *The Merchant of Venice* that has consistently been propped up to show how Shakespeare calls on us to treat others humanely, or a play like *King Lear* where the one deemed illegitimate thoughtfully interrogates the unjust and arbitrary nature of customs that label certain individuals inferior simply by nature of their birth? Indeed, as I say early on in this chapter, Shylock's iconic "Hath not a Jew eyes?" (3.1.53) speech is seen as a touchstone for those seeking to humanize foreigners. However, his speech fails to resonate with the racists within the play. As soon as Shylock's words are spoken, Tubal enters and Salanio remarks, "Here comes another of the tribe; a third cannot be matched, unless the devil himself turn Jew" (3.1.70–71). In the minds of the many racists within the play—and within Shakespeare's England, we can safely assume—Jews, like Black individuals, are likened to the devil.[25] We know, however, that the true evil resides elsewhere in that play. But not many of us are willing to interrogate that whiteness.

Racism abounds in *The Merchant of Venice*, but it is Portia who stands out to me in this regard not only because of her desire to strip Shylock of all autonomy in the courtroom scene but also because of her general view of those who are not white. Before she intercedes on behalf of her rich, white counterparts in the play, she has already made her feelings clear about those who do not resemble her own. She says of the suitor Morocco choosing the incorrect casket, "A gentle riddance! Draw the curtains, go. / Let all of his complexion choose me so" (2.7.86–7). She has no desire to be close to those whose skin is dark. When she enters the courtroom to serve as the arbiter of justice, her white rage is put on full display for us to see. There is no impartiality in place, and unfortunately that rings true in our own justice system when it comes to the discrepancy between the adjudication of crimes committed by Black and brown individuals versus white individuals. In *The Merchant of Venice*, the verdict is unjust, if only because Shylock is stripped not only of property but also of fundamental dignity simply because he is an "alien" (4.1.364). It isn't enough that he does not get his pound of flesh, because Portia as Balthasar, representing the state, makes sure that she can make an example of that ambitious Jew.

Rather than argue that *The Merchant of Venice* shows that Shakespeare favored immigrants, then, perhaps we ought to see that the play in fact unveils to its audience their own complicity in systems that consistently favor whiteness above all else.[26] Nobody pushes back. Nobody speaks on behalf of Shylock. He humanizes himself to an audience who does not see him as human—not before his speech nor after. For people of color, that is a concept with cross-historical implications, as one could very well make that same argument about so many Black and brown people in our society today. Maybe we ought not to emphasize Shylock's compelling appeal to his racist audience in Act 3 as a hopeful layer to this play, but instead look straightforwardly and critically at the white racist society in which he still resides in Act 5. To behold that monstrosity—to see that the Merchant of Venice is actually a racist white man who is proud of spitting on Shylock because he is a Jew (1.3.141), and whose racist white community rallies behind him—would perhaps compel us to adopt anti-racist attitudes, pedagogies, and if we are willing to go as far as Friar Madden wanted his community in North Carolina to go, policies. I think the key is to look at and make visible this kind of vicious whiteness.

It is the complicity to abide by understood hierarchies, behaviors, and attitudes that imagine whiteness as superior that we should interrogate forcefully. George Lipsitz suggests that "whiteness is a matter of interests as well as attitudes" and goes on to argue that "the possessive investment in whiteness is a matter of behavior as well as belief."[27] As I come to a close in this chapter, then, I want to consider Shakespeare's imagining of behaviors and beliefs that define the nascent Englishness in his history play, *Henry V*, because it is a play that, without doubt, invites us to look straightforwardly at such constructions of whiteness. The jingoism that runs throughout that play is meant to inspire its English audience to imagine itself as being a part of the "few," "the happy few," the "band of brothers" (4.1.62) of Henry's imagination. However, for all of Henry's inspiring speeches, it is the bookends of that play that capture the dangerous ethnocentrism and exclusionary measures behind such imaginings.

When the Bishop of Ely and the Bishop of Canterbury explore King Henry V's transformation into a dignified leader—a transformation where his "body" is now imagined as a "paradise / T' envelop and contain celestial spirits" (1.1.32–3)—the audience is asked to imagine the king, and by implication his kingdom, as metaphorically divine. Saturated in hyperbole, the opening scenes establish Henry's superior nature, but it also sets the stage to articulate with clarity how such superiority is able to flourish. Ely says: "The strawberry grows underneath the nettle, / And wholesome berries thrive and ripen best / Neighbored by fruit of baser quality" (1.1.63–5). Here, Ely is contemplating Henry's growth when he was surrounded by the likes of Falstaff in the previous plays of the Henriad. However, this idea is later applicable to England itself when Henry and his fellow noblemen consider the "pilfering borderers," "giddy neighbors," and general "ill neighborhood" that threaten their nation (1.2.148, 152, 160). It is against that "fruit of baser quality" that England will thrive.

As in the case with *King Lear*, defining who is "base" allows the English in *Henry V* to establish who is superior, and at every turn, they imagine the English as vastly superior. When the Chorus imagines England as a "model to thy inward greatness, / Like little body with a mighty heart," it adds the caveat, "What might'st thou do, that honor would thee do, / Were all thy children kind and natural" (2.0.16–19). The explicit reference is to a group of traitorous English noblemen—Lord Scroop of Masham, Sir Thomas Grey, and the Earl of Cambridge—but the play also deploys language of legitimacy, as "kind" and "natural" connote clear notions of similitude. If England were homogenous, how much greater would it be? The phrase "inward greatness" resonates loudly when we consider how the word "great" has been deployed in our present moment in the United States. To be kind and natural is to belong, and not all citizens—in Shakespeare's England, in his plays, and in our own world—are thought to belong. To many, the phrase "make America great again" means that we ought to make America white again.

More menacing, to my mind though, is the way the play imagines a larger Eurocentric community at the play's end. When Henry finishes his coercive courting of Katherine, he says to her, "Shall not thou and I, between Saint Denis and Saint George, compound a boy, half French, half English, that shall go to Constantinople and take the Turk by the beard?" (5.2.215–17). I readily recognize the gesture here at a type of Christian, masculine-centered community that the English (via the French Katherine) stand to organize, but the evocation of the Turk as not only a point of contrast for that Christian kinship but as the fearful foreigner who must be the perpetual target of violence brings forth a kind of malicious need to elevate whiteness through the disparagement of those unalike. This is what white supremacy demands.

At the play's close, the chorus reminds the audience that that bold, Christian, half English, half French, white child of Henry's imagination actually reigns over a nation that endures years of civil unrest all because the English fight among their own kind (with no Turk in sight). Still, even the final line of *Henry V*—"In your fair minds let this acceptance take" (Epilogue, 14)— evokes what Kim F. Hall describes as the "emergent ideology of white supremacy" through its description of those English minds as "fair."[28] The play espouses aspirations for nation building and empire, but when it comes to those who are not alike, any sense of kinship or kindness falls by the wayside. That is what empire calls for— human capital and a system where those dark of skin are, at every single turn, rendered illegitimate and expendable. When it comes to those not fair of skin, not Christian, or not like them, Christian kindness ultimately and always gives way to shotguns.

NOTES

1 Luis Alberto Urrea, *The Devil's Highway* (New York: Back Bay Books, 2014), 221.

2 Ibid., 229.

3 See www.youtube.com/watch?v=yfvXNOuGkig

4 See www.chathamnc.org/home/showdocument?id=8735

5 See www.azleg.gov/legtext/49leg/2r/bills/sb1070s.pdf. Arizona Senate Bill 1070, of course, passed into law and spurred debate about immigrants' rights. The danger, as many saw it, was the blatantly xenophobic nature behind the law. The American Civil Liberties Union argues that because of this law passed in 2010, almost two dozen copy cat laws around the United States were introduced: "laws inspired by Arizona's SB 1070 invite rampant racial profiling against Latinos, Asian-Americans and others presumed to be 'foreign' based on how they look or sound. They also authorize police to demand papers proving citizenship or immigration status from anyone they stop and suspect of being in the country unlawfully" (www.aclu.org/arizonas-sb-1070). To date, the debate about immigration continues, with many calling for widespread reform so as to protect undocumented immigrants in the United States.

6 William Shakespeare, *The Merchant of Venice*, ed. Barbara Mowat and Paul Werstine (New York: Folger Shakespeare Library, 2010).

7 See www.youtube.com/watch?v=yfvXNOuGkig

8 "The Strangers' Case—Shakespeare's Rallying Cry for Humanity," International Rescue Committee & Shakespeare's Globe, June 20, 2018. www.youtube.com/watch?v=4Bss2or4n74

9 Anthony Munday, Henry Chettle, Thomas Dekker, Thomas Heywood, and William Shakespeare, *Sir Thomas More*, ed. John Jowett (London: Arden Shakespeare, 2011).

10 "The Strangers' Case."

11 Scott Warren, "I gave water to migrants crossing the Arizona desert. They charged me with a felony," *Washington Post*, May 28, 2019. www.washingtonpost.com/outlook/2019/05/28/i-gave-water-migrants-crossing-arizona-desert-they-charged-me-with-felony/

12 For this story, see, "9:25am—Dead Mom Dragged Across Desert," *Albuquerque Journal*, August 2, 2006. www.abqjournal.com/22966/925am-dead-mom-dragged-across-desert.html

13 Sasha Pimentel, *For Want of Water* (Boston: Beacon Press, 2017), 49.

14 Ibid., 49.

15 Ibid., 49. ´

16 Ibid., 50.

17 William Shakespeare, *King Lear*, ed. Barbara A. Mowat and Paul Werstine (New York: Folger Shakespeare Library, 1993).

18 In fact, this example from *The Merchant of Venice* is listed under the etymology for "nation" in the *Oxford English Dictionary* (1.a).

19 William Shakespeare, *Henry V*, ed. Barbara A. Mowat and Paul Werstine (New York: Folger Shakespeare Library, 1995).

20 Here, I clearly have in mind Benedict Anderson's *Imagined Communities: Reflections on the Origin and Spread of Nationalism* (London: Verso, 1983).

21 Carol Anderson, *White Rage: The Unspoken Truth of Our Racial Divide* (New York: Bloomsbury, 2016), 3.

22 Ibid., 3.

23 Bill Hutchinson, Aaron Katersky, and Josh Margolin, "Alleged Shooter Cased El Paso Walmart Before Rampage That Killed 22: Law Enforcement Officials," *ABC News*, August 5, 2019. https://abcnews.go.com/US/death-toll-rises-22-el-paso-shooting-victims/story?id=64780680. See also Robert Moore and Mark Berman, "El Paso Suspect Said he Was Targeting 'Mexicans,' Told Officers He Was the Shooter, Police Say," *The Washington Post*, August 9, 2019. www.washingtonpost.com/national/el-paso-suspect-said-he-was-targeting-mexicans-told-officers-he-was-the-shooter-police-say/2019/08/09/ab235e18-bac9-11e9-b3b4-2bb69e8c4e39_story.html

24 I have in mind here George Lipsitz, *The Possessive Investment in Whiteness: How White People Profit from Identity Politics* (Philadelphia: Temple UP, 1998), esp. 99.

25 For anti-Semitic attitudes in Shakespeare's England, see James Shapiro, *Shakespeare and the Jews* (New York: Columbia UP, 1997).

26 For a brilliant reading of the paradigm in *The Merchant of Venice* that favors white, elite men, see Kim Hall, "Guess Who's Coming to Dinner? Colonization and Miscegenation in *The Merchant of Venice*," *Renaissance Drama* 23.1, esp. 100.

27 Lipsitz, 233.

28 Kim Hall, "'These bastard signs of fair': Literary Whiteness in Shakespeare's Sonnets," *Post-Colonial Shakespeares*, ed. Ania Loomba and Martin Orkin (London: Routledge, 1998), 67.

Three

The NPR editor's note introducing an article about a young Syrian boy named Aylan Kurdi reads, "The photos in this story may be distressing to some viewers."[1] I begin with this editor's note because the idea that "some viewers" would not find photographs of the lifeless body of a three-year-old boy distressing is, in itself, distressing. The image of this young boy, face down on the sandy shores of Turkey, served as a testament to the suffering that so many Syrian refugees faced as they tried to escape the turmoil and violence of their homeland in hopes of finding safety. The mere thought of that image is devastatingly heartbreaking. Despite the fact that upwards of four million Syrians had fled the country prior to the publication of this photograph in 2015, it was this image of Aylan Kurdi that sparked outrage and attention to the plight of so many. Diane Cole, the author of the 2017 NPR article, asks, what was the impact of that photo? The answer to that question is not so simple.

Cole considers how this photo in particular caught the world's attention and draws on a study that examines what lasting influence it had. As one might expect, the greatest impact came in the way of a surge in donations to agencies committed to aiding Syrian refugees. The image of that dead child was so distressing that viewers felt compelled to act. As Cole states, this "single photo of a single individual" had the potency to "stir the emotions and arouse public concerns more powerfully than statistical reports of body counts," which was already in the hundreds of thousands when the article was written, and by 2020 had reached approximately 400,000.[2] Let that sink in. Four hundred thousand human lives lost. But it was the image of a single boy that provoked a compassionate reaction to the crisis. It should. However, one should also wonder why so many of us were not paying attention to all the other lives lost.

Most of us know that the U.S. response to the Syrian crisis was tepid at first, and fundamentally inhumane thereafter. The Trump administration signed an executive order in 2017 banning noncitizens from seven Muslim-majority nations, including Syria, from entering the United States. It was one in a long line of xenophobic and racist policies that the administration put forward. In the process, Trump was able to mobilize an anti-immigrant and Islamophobic base by espousing views that his xenophobic policies would preserve the integrity of our nation and keep us safe. If he had touted his ability to build a wall along the U.S. Mexico border and have Mexico pay for it, here he was simply saying that Muslims are not welcome. For Trump and his base, the image of Aylan Kurdi clearly meant nothing. Perhaps to them, he was merely one more dead foreigner. Maybe they are the NPR readers who don't find the image of a dead child distressing. All the while, the Syrian crisis continues as the images of dying children fade into the background.

This chapter considers how images and voices of children often hold the most power in drawing attention to the injustices that those seeking refuge, asylum, or even fundamental belonging often face. These images matter, not just because behind them one sees a promise left unrealized, but also because through them we understand the viciousness of the reach of racist and tyrannical structures. The latter is something that Shakespeare's work often explores. Whether it be young princes being taken to their certain death in the Tower of London in *Richard III*, Macduff processing the news of the murder of his children in *Macbeth*, the announcement of Mamillius' death and the abandonment of Perdita in *The Winter's Tale*, or the orders for Aaron to murder his newborn son in *Titus Andronicus*, Shakespeare sometimes deploys images of suffering and murdered innocent children to convey the horrors of tyranny. Without doubt, Shakespeare's work capitalizes on the valence of such imagery and its potential to impact audiences. As Camillo says of the young Prince Mamillius at the opening of *The Winter's Tale*, "It is a gallant child; one that, indeed, physics the subject, makes old hearts fresh" (1.1.40–1).[3] In Sicilia, Mamillius is seen as a cure to the ills and old age of that society. He is the promise of a better future for those people. When a child suffers an untimely death, then, such promise is broken.

In our present moment, the truth is that so many children of immigration persist and live suffering in the shadows of societies that offer little sanctuary or security. It is a precarious existence because a "return" to their homeland is actually a return to a land many of them have never truly known. Such is the case for many undocumented individuals who have lived the better part of their lives in the United States, and who are part of the Deferred Action for Childhood Arrival (DACA) initiative. This initiative seeks to allow young adults who arrived in the United States as undocumented children to attend school or work lawfully without fear of deportation as they await a lawful path to citizenship. With all their anti-immigrant bluster in place, the Trump administration sought to end this initiative in 2017. The Trump administration was challenged in court after rescinding this program, and the Supreme Court ultimately ruled against Trump. Make no mistake about it, the idea was to have as many Latinxs as possible expelled from the land they call home under the premise that they had broken the law. The majority of these Latinx immigrants arrived with their parents and had absolutely no clue about our stringent immigration laws. We can safely assume, too, that the better part of their lives they must have consistently felt like outsiders living in a land that did not want them.

To consider these vulnerable children in particular, then, is to recognize our failings from generation to generation. The path to citizenship in the United States is not easy for most immigrants, and thus those who have come here to search for stability and a chance at a decent life often confront the consistent fear of deportation. Moreover, a sizable portion of the U.S. population simply sees in those children who are not white a future threat to their existence. Despite the pathos behind the image of three-year-old Aylan Kurdi mentioned above, resistance to Syrian refugees and other immigrants remains. Our failure persists.

On a fundamental level, it should be easy to recognize why confronting the reality of a suffering child should matter. The children are not at fault for the cruelty of the world that surrounds them. As Paulina says of Hermione's newborn child, Perdita, in *The Winter's Tale*:

> The child was prisoner to the womb, and is
> By law and process of great nature thence

> Freed and enfranchised, not a party to
> The anger of the King, nor guilty of,
> If any be, the trespass of the Queen.
>
> (2.3.72–6)

This, of course, comes after Leontes' tyrannical move to imprison Hermione, his wife, because he suspects her of infidelity. Paulina, though, takes it upon herself to give voice to the innocent child and to argue on her behalf. She recognizes that the child will suffer unless the tyranny is addressed. In this way, Shakespeare allows us to consider the oppressive structures—defined here by patriarchal control and toxic masculinity—that will inevitably influence the experiences of children, and also invites us to think about the way to resist such structures. Indeed, fighting for a secure environment for children ought to be central when we consider our ethical responsibilities to each other.

To be absolutely clear, in our present moment, we need to consider our complicity in social structures that so often impede positive experiences for Black and brown children. We need to consider that what some people see in those Black and brown children is far less than what they see in their white counterparts. And by some people, I mean teachers, school administrators, health professionals, police officers, cashiers, school bus drivers, parents at playgrounds, and so many more. Everyday lived experiences for Black and brown children are impacted by these shades of racism. To look earnestly at the way our society cares for Black and brown children is akin to looking at Leontes and recognizing the absolute lack of care or compassion for his own newborn child. How do we feel about our children, treat our children, all of our children, in the United States?

To get to a closer examination of this issue, I want to think about the way Shakespeare draws on children to underscore the violent and oppressive realities of the world in which they reside. Take, for example, the way children are imagined in *Macbeth*. On the one hand, we should consider how the Weyward Sisters make it a point to say that although Macbeth will be king, it is Banquo who will beget kings.[4] Children become a focal point because they exist as the vehicle for the legacy of their fathers. As in the case of the imagined child of Henry's imagination in *Henry V* that I discussed in the previous chapter, children can be seen as a continuation of the father's desire to rule and to conquer—to reign supreme, as it were. In *Macbeth*, it is the threat of Banquo's *children* that leads Macbeth to have him murdered. Lest we forget, he intends to have Banquo murdered, but also makes it clear to the murderers that Banquo's young son, Fleance, must also "embrace the fate / Of that dark hour" (3.1.156–7). It is Fleance in particular who poses the biggest threat to Macbeth's legacy, and so he becomes a target. The play, then, puts forward an order for a child to be murdered.

So, what is the correlation between the view of children in a play like *Macbeth* and views of children in our own present-day society? Because *Macbeth* interrogates what it means to be a man (not only in gendered imaginings but also in regard to one's humanity) and the fundamental value of hospitality in the face of a violent and tyrannical world, I think compelling connections surface. I will return to the former topic of "man" later in this chapter, but here I want to consider why the latter notion of hospitality in the play holds contemporary relevance for us as we consider the welfare (or lack thereof) of children in our society.

Before Lady Macbeth and Macbeth contemplate the killing of Duncan, Macbeth acknowledges the moral imperatives that ought to be guiding his thinking. He is trying to make sense of his ethical responsibilities as Duncan's host. Macbeth says of Duncan:

> He's here in double trust:
> First, as I am his kinsman and subject,
> Strong both against the deed; then, as his host,
> Who should against his murderer shut the door,
> Not bear the knife myself... .

(1.7.12–16)

Macbeth ultimately violates that double trust, as he betrays Duncan as kinsman and subject, and does indeed bear the knife to kill his guest. It is a heinous act that violates all principles of hospitality. But that, I think, is the point. The play offers the nightmarish view of Macbeth's rule because no one is safe in an inhospitable world—not even young children, as we eventually see. Such a violent, inhospitable space is the hell of the Porter's imagination. This premise of the dangers of inhospitality should guide the way we think about the play, and the way we think about the world in which we live.

That very notion of inhospitality governs so many attitudes about Black and brown people in our society today, and, as in the case of *Macbeth*, children suffer severely in the face of such oppressive, inhospitable structures. To consider then, as I did in the previous two chapters, how our society views Blacks and Latinxs allows us to recognize the fundamental absence of an ethics of hospitality for so many in our nation. This inhospitality stems beyond the idea of making someone feel unwelcome, but rather it creates and sustains a belief that certain people have ownership over this nation while others are perpetual guests here. Donald J. Trump, for example, said that congresswomen Alexandra Ocasio-Cortez, Ilhan Omar, Rashida Tlaib, and Ayanna S. Pressley should "go back" to the countries from which they came.[5] All four congresswomen are women of color, and three of the four were born in the United States. It is hardly difficult to arrive at the conclusion that Trump sees non-whites as foreign to this nation. But of course, it isn't just Trump who thinks this way. So many U.S. citizens continue to see those darker of skin as guests in this country—guests who can and should be sent "back" to wherever they came from if they fail to adopt the dominant ideologies of this nation. For those who think this way, of course, such dominant ideologies are rooted in white supremacy.

The majority of Black and Latinx children are not foreign to this nation. The United States belongs to them and they belong to it, no matter how often they are made to feel that this is not the case by so many of our nation's white leaders. But when young Black or brown children see themselves reflected in their leaders, then conceivably something powerful can happen, right? Because this chapter is concerned with images and voices of children, I attend here to an iconic image of a young Black boy visiting the Oval Office at the White House. In that photograph, President Barack Obama bends forward as the boy's arm is outstretched and his hand is placed on President Obama's hair. It is, without doubt, a tender image to behold. The story goes that the young boy, Jacob Philadelphia, was offered the opportunity to ask President Obama one question. Jacob said, "I want to know if my hair is just like yours," to which President Obama answered, "Why don't you touch it and see for yourself?" When Jacob hesitated, President Obama encouraged him: "Touch it, dude!"[6] Jacob came to find that it did, indeed, feel the same.

That image, loaded with so much meaning, opens the door for us to consider the inhospitality that our nation so often offers. On the one hand, what must it mean for a young Black boy to be in the Oval Office and see in the President of the United States skin and hair that looks like his own? Conversely, how is that young boy defined by the world around him because of the color of his skin and the texture of his hair? In that moment of belonging for that young boy, we are all also made vividly aware of the tremendous weight of unbelonging. If only for a moment, though, that young boy's president was Black.

The long history of positing Black U.S. citizens as outsiders in this country has calcified over time. In that image, we behold a President who, because he is Black, was also thought to be a foreigner—the sole target of the "birther movement" supported by no other than Trump, the man who ultimately became his successor. As Ta-Nehisi Coates writes of Trump, "His political career began in advocacy of birtherism, that modern recasting of the old American precept that black people are not fit to be citizens of the country they built. But long before birtherism, Trump had made his worldview clear."[7] That worldview, of course, included housing discrimination against Blacks, a public appeal that called for the death penalty for the ultimately exonerated Central Park Five (five black teenagers unjustly accused of raping a white woman), casting Mexicans as rapists and murderers, and an undeniable affinity for white supremacists. This is because, as Coates suggest, Trump's "ideology is white supremacy, in all its truculent and sanctimonious power."[8]

So, to consider that young boy admiring President Obama, feeling in the texture of the President's hair his own, and then to realize that this young boy will grow to be a young Black man inhabiting the kind of world that sees him as unfit to be a U.S. citizen—a kind of world where Trump's racism goes unchecked—is absolutely appalling. As Coates goes on to say about Trump:

> To Trump, whiteness is neither notional nor symbolic but is the very core of his power. In this, Trump is not singular. But whereas his forebears carried whiteness like an ancestral talisman, Trump cracked the glowing amulet open, releasing its eldritch energies. The repercussions are striking: Trump is the first president to have served in no public capacity before ascending to his perch. But more telling, Trump is also the first president to have publicly affirmed that his daughter is a "piece of ass." The mind seizes trying to imagine a black man extolling the virtues of sexual assault on tape ("When you're a star, they let you do it"), fending off multiple accusations of such assaults, immersed in multiple lawsuits for allegedly fraudulent business dealings, exhorting his followers to violence, and then strolling into the White House. But that is the point of white supremacy—to ensure that that which all others achieve with maximal effort, white people (particularly men) achieve with minimal qualification. Barack Obama delivered to black people the hoary message that if they work twice as hard as white people, anything is possible. But Trump's counter is persuasive: Work half as hard as black people, and even more is possible.[9]

In so many ways, Trump himself serves as the counterimage to the powerful photograph of the young Jacob reaching out to feel President Obama's hair. You are likely expecting a joke about hair here, but that is not at all my intent. In Obama's reaction to that young boy, we locate something humane, and in the image of Trump the man, we see only callousness. Coates is clear that the only reason Trump is in the White House is that structures of white supremacy have allowed for that. At every turn, he has given voters every single reason to see that he is in no way qualified to lead, that his behavior and actions have been nothing short of reprehensible, and yet there he is, an elected president in the White House. For those who are not white, the horror of that image is deeply unsettling. How do you explain to a young Black or brown child that so many of their fellow citizens found him fit for office?

The injustice and inhospitable ethos of a nation under Trump stems far beyond the fact that this young Black boy will grow to be a young Black man in a country where the color of his skin will put him in grave danger. We need only consider the separation of families at the U.S. Mexico border, and the incarceration of immigrant children in detention centers to recognize that an "unwelcome" sign is always in place for Black and brown people in the United States. As many have argued, it is true that stringent immigration policies were in place long before Trump. However, the separation of families at the border is the sinister work of his administration, with Stephen Miller as the catalyst for this inhumane program.[10] I should be clear in noting here, though, that so many enabled Trump to put this awful program into effect. And I don't mean just those who voted for him. So many members of congress have stood behind Trump either cheering him on or in silence, and that is terrifying. Should we, then, logically assume that Trump's racist America is what they also want?

When early images of children being kept in cages while in custody of U.S. Customs and Border Protection (CBP) were first published, the public outcry was swift and similar to the public reaction to the image of Aylan Kurdi surfacing. Slowly, stories from these inhumane migrant children's detention centers began to emerge, and an audio of a young crying child in one of these centers was leaked. In the audio attained by ProPublica, the crying of several children is heard in the background while a Border Patrol agent jokes, in Spanish no less, that what this "orchestra" needs is a "conductor."[11] In direct opposition to that inhumane comment is the voice of a six-year-old Salvadoran girl who "pleads repeatedly for someone to call her aunt. Just one call, she begs anyone who will listen. She says she's memorized the phone number, and at one point, rattles it off to a consular representative. 'My mommy says that I'll go with my aunt,' she whimpers, 'and that she'll come to pick me up there as quickly as possible.'"[12] In the background, you can hear a younger child repeatedly calling for her daddy. The sound of these children crying is absolutely agonizing. With inhumane actions like this transpiring on U.S. soil at the hands of U.S. government officials, we no longer have any ground to stand on to castigate foreign nations for human rights abuses. The truth is, this nation has always trafficked in human rights abuses, as our long history of racist violence demonstrates. It happens year after year after year.

What is categorically unforgivable about all of this is that the indefinite detainment of children crossing the border is not a legal necessity. In a recent interview with PBS News Hour, Warren Binford, a lawyer who conducted interviews at a migrant children's detention center in Clint, Texas, offers a succinct explanation of what Immigration and Customs Enforcement (ICE) and CBP are doing:

And so basically, what we're doing is, we're taking children away from their family at the border. We're putting them in inhumane conditions in Border Patrol facilities, where they shouldn't be at all, not even for a few hours. And that 72 hours, that's the maximum that someone is supposed to be kept there.[13]

Binford makes clear that in those facilities, "dirty children who are malnourished" and "severely neglected" are "essentially being warehoused"—"as many as 300 children in a cell, with almost no adult supervision."[14] How can anyone try to justify such abuse?

If one is perhaps trying to be "objective" by employing the tired excuse that these children came illegally (when most of them actually came legally seeking refuge), one might ask, "well, where are they supposed to send these children?" In answering that question, we can easily identify the nefarious nature of the way the Trump administration is handling this. Binford continues:

Almost none of the children that we interviewed had come across the border themselves alone. Essentially, they came across the border with family. And they are trying to be reunited with family who are living in the United States. Almost every child that I interviewed had family, parents, uncles, aunts, grandparents, siblings here in the United States who are waiting for them and are ready to care for them.[15]

Instead of placing these young children with family members who could adequately care for them while their cases make their way through the immigration courts, these privately run facilities are making money hand over fist by detaining these children indefinitely in utterly inhumane conditions. "We have children caring for other young children," Binford says, and describes a two-year old without diapers who urinated in the care of another child. When Binford asked a CBP employee why this child didn't have diapers, she was told the child didn't need it. She continues:

> The children are hardly being fed anything nutritious, and they are being medically neglected. We're seeing a flu outbreak, and we're also seeing a lice infestation. It is—we have children sleeping on the floor. It's the worst conditions I have ever witnessed in several years of doing these inspections.[16]

And Binford is unequivocal in explaining that keeping the children in these facilities is "not required by law. That's just the way the administration is doing it. These children can be placed with their families immediately, if we wanted to do that." Clearly, they do not want to do that. I'm tempted to follow this by writing: the question is, why? However, the answer to that is obvious. We know that brown children are devalued beyond belief in our nation. We know that this administration has absolutely no regard for these children in detention centers. We know that, given the choice, they would choose a shotgun over water ten times out of ten. The handling of these children is rooted in racism and the administration has demonstrated a fundamental absence of humanity. But how invested is the average U.S. citizen in the lives of these brown children? What is our level of complicity within this awful system?

This attention to inhumane structures, then, is where I locate a poignant connection to Shakespeare. When *Macbeth* offers a glimpse of a lighthearted exchange between

Lady Macduff and her young son, whom she endearingly calls "poor monkey" and "poor prattler" (4.2.65, 70), we witness something surprisingly tender during an otherwise frightening depiction of that world. The exchange doesn't overtly provoke our pity, but rather offers an amusing repartee to demonstrate, quite subtly, the trust and bond this mother and son share. They are both witty, and playful, and seemingly positive despite the tyrannous backdrop of the play. But it is also a scene that contains within it both a mother's love for, and the murder of, that child.

The willingness to murder children illustrates the extent to which Macbeth will go to maintain power and secure his legacy. There is no bottom to that cruelty. One could easily argue that this is exactly how white supremacy works in its own investments in power and legacy. The incarceration of brown children coming to the U.S. Mexico border is monstrous, but what is equally horrific is that such unnecessary tactics are meant to exhibit and sustain the perception of white supremacy because the lives of these brown children are imagined as expendable. It is not merely a message to say to them, "you do not belong here," but to say to all of us dark of skin, "we can and will do this to you and to yours." And what can Shakespeare teach us about this cruelty? Nothing. He can teach us absolutely nothing about this. We don't need Shakespeare to recognize that cruelty. He doesn't contain some universal truth to shine a spotlight on that horror. But what we can perhaps recognize is that there is an opportunity to understand that when I—brown of skin and disheartened that my people are kept in camps just miles from my hometown— bring particular experiences to the table when engaging with and putting the spotlight on Shakespeare, his works mean something very different. That difference, I think, is critical to behold and to treat with seriousness whenever we consider how scholars and readers who are Black, Indigenous, and People of Color (BIPOC) come at Shakespeare. What we make of Shakespeare stands to cast a light on the shades of racism that surround us.

Where I locate poignancy in *Macbeth* when considering how Black and brown children in our world are devalued is in Macduff's response to the news of the murder of his wife and children. It is as heartbreaking a moment as you'll find in all of Shakespeare's oeuvre. Ross enters and interrupts the conversation between Macduff and Malcolm, and the latter asks, "What's the newest grief?" (4.3.200). Ross, understandably apprehensive to reveal to Macduff that his family has been murdered, stalls in revealing that particular news. When pressed, he finally says:

> Your castle is surprised, your wife and babes
> Savagely slaughtered. To relate the manner
> Were on the quarry of these murdered deer
> To add the death of you.
>
> (4.3.2400–43)

Macduff struggles to speak, but ultimately asks, "My children too?" Clearly, he is in disbelief. But he needs to know. The conversation continues:

> Ross: Wife, children, servants, all that could be found.
> Macduff: And I must be from thence? My wife killed too?
> Ross: I have said.
> Malcolm: Be comforted.
>   Let's make us med'cines of our great revenge.
>   To cure this deadly grief.

Macduff: He has no children. All my pretty ones?
   Did you say "all"? O hell-kite! All?
   What, all my pretty chickens and their dam
   At one fell swoop?
Malcolm: Dispute it like a man.
Macduff: I shall do so.
   But I must also feel it as a man.

(4.3.249–61)

Urged to enact revenge on Macbeth for killing his wife and children, Macduff instead pauses to recognize and feel the weight of this loss. "All my pretty ones?" he asks. What we as an audience are asked to apprehend here is not only the loss that this father feels but also the violent world that does not cease. Malcolm immediately sees revenge as the cure to Macduff's grief. He prods Macduff to act on that grief—to dispute it as a man should. Macduff's rejoinder, "But I must also feel it as a man," echoes loudly the play's attention to the absence of humanity in the world of *Macbeth*. As a human, Macduff needs to feel this pain and he is clearly asking others to empathize with him. When he asks, then, "All my pretty ones?" they are not his alone. These children are the responsibility of all of us. We must all feel that loss, we must all feel that pain, and thereafter, as Macduff does, we must all act on it.

When the terrorist Patrick Crusius, whom I discussed in the previous chapter, traveled across Texas from Dallas to El Paso, he drove past the town of Clint. The particular migrant children's detention center featured on the PBS News Hour segment that I discussed above is located in Clint, a town that is a mere 30-minute drive from El Paso. When the

Walmart massacre was over, an outpouring of both local and national support and sympathy quickly washed over the El Paso community. The national media descended on El Paso, and the sorrow of this city was on the nightly news. People were angry, sad, shaken, and overall quick to offer whatever support they could to the families of the victims. The slogan, "El Paso Strong" was adopted city wide. The local community came together, and the broader U.S. community looked on in seeming solidarity. Still, 30 minutes away, kids were in cages and whatever anger anyone was feeling about that situation was muted.

The media connected the terrorist act with the incendiary remarks of Trump and later to Texas Governor Greg Abbot, who before the shooting had called on Texans to "defend" the border.[17] But directly after the massacre, Abbot traveled to El Paso, was welcomed into a church that my mother attended the better part of her life, and prayed alongside our community—most of whom are of Mexican descent. I found Abbot's presence in my hometown revolting, as his policies are aligned with those of Trump. Indeed, when Trump enacted the so-called Muslim ban, Abbot forcefully supported this policy and made it clear that Texas would not accept any Syrian refugees. Clearly, the man knows nothing about the way U.S. immigration law works, but I digress. What Abbot was obviously trying to do is to signal to the constituents who voted him into office that he believed Texas should remain majority white. It was no different than him calling for Texans to "defend" the border. Understandably, the story was that Crusius was influenced by the political tone from the top that harnessed hatred toward Latinxs. But before Crusius shot one single bullet, brown kids in camps were already dying, and our government was responsible. Still, those children remain within detention centers in Texas. Who will say of these brown children, "All my pretty ones?" After all, isn't this our collective responsibility?

The heartlessness behind the child migrant detention centers breaks my heart because it is not unlike the horrors and tyranny of *Macbeth*. It is not unlike the horror behind the actions of a group of men willing to tear an unborn baby out of a lynched mother's womb and killing that crying baby with their boot heels. It is the most horrific ends of racism that we can imagine, and it transpires here day after day. To think of Macbeth's "Tomorrow" speech with these incarcerated children in mind is to understand the terror at recognizing the futility of asking others to care just a bit more about these children:

> Tomorrow and tomorrow and tomorrow
> Creeps in this petty pace from day to day
> To the last syllable of recorded time,
> And all our yesterdays have lighted fools
> The way to dusty death. Out, out, brief candle!
> Life's but a walking shadow, a poor player
> That struts and frets his hour upon the stage
> And then is heard no more. It is a tale
> Told by an idiot, full of sound and fury
> Signifying nothing.

(5.5.22–31)

With the structures of white supremacy that have allowed for these family separations in mind, it is difficult not to recognize in this speech the long tradition of enduring—a habit that so many who do not approximate whiteness face within this nation, within this land of the free, where structures of racism again and again devalue us and render our lives less important than.

Amid this critique of the manifold shortcomings of our nation when it comes to human rights abuses, I readily recognize that many will ask why I am here. Many will assume I lack patriotism. I'm too exhausted to defend myself, but I will simply say that this America is the only home I have ever known and ever loved, and I want it to be better. I won't lie, the racist violence that our nation has shown itself capable of enacting is the most frightening facet of this homeland. Indeed, when Lady Macbeth claims that, had she made such a promise, she would dash "the brains out" of a smiling baby after plucking its gums from her nipple, the audience is asked to behold the horror of that image (1.7.66). In the case of Mary Turner, that image was made real. Amid tyranny, and amid the capacity for such violent racism, no child is safe. Not one. And thus, all our pretty ones are susceptible when a nation keeps even one child in a cage. This fact should be distressing to all of us. We can't simply look on and then look away. We must act and recognize, as Siward does in *Macbeth*, that "certain issues strokes must arbitrate" (5.4.26). We must feel it in a humane way, and then we must work deliberately and collectively to dismantle such racist paradigms and threats of tyranny.

NOTES

1 Diane Cole, "Study: What Was the Impact of the Iconic Photo of the Syrian Boy?" NPR, January 13, 2017. www.npr.org/sections/goatsandsoda/2017/01/13/509650251/study-what-was-the-impact-of-the-iconic-photo-of-the-syrian-boy

2 Ibid. See also, "Syrian Civil War Fast Facts," CNN, April 9, 2020. www. cnn.com/2013/08/27/world/meast/syria-civil-war-fast-facts/ index.html

3 William Shakespeare, *The Winter's Tale*, ed. Barbara A. Mowat and Paul Werstine (New York: Folger Shakespeare Library, 1998).

4 For the use of "weyward" as opposed to "weird," see Ayanna Thompson, "What is a 'Weyward' *Macbeth*," *Weyward Macbeth: Intersections of Race and Performance* (New York: Palgrave, 2010): 3–10.

5 Katie Rogers and Nicholas Fandos, "Trump Tells Congresswomen to 'Go Back' to the Countries They Came From," *New York Times*, July 14, 2019. www.nytimes.com/2019/07/14/us/politics/trump-twitter-squad-congress.html

6 Jackie Calmes, "When a Boy Felt a Familiar Feel in a Pat of the Head of State," *The New York Times*, May 23, 2012. www.nytimes.com/2012/ 05/24/us/politics/indelible-image-of-a-boys-pat-on-obamas-head-hangs-in-white-house.html

7 Ta-Nehisi Coates, "The First White President," *The Atlantic*, October 2017. www.theatlantic.com/magazine/archive/2017/10/the-first-white-president-ta-nehisi-coates/537909/?utm_source=atlfb

8 Ibid.

9 Ibid.

10 For more on the origin of the policies to separate families at the U.S. Mexico border, see, Michael D. Shear, Katie Benner, and Michael S. Schmidt, "'We Need to Take Away Children, 'No Matter How Young,' Justice Department Officials Said," *New York Times*, October 6, 2020. www.nytimes.com/2020/10/06/us/politics/family-separation-border-immigration-jeff-sessions-rod-rosenstein.html

11 Ginger Thompson, "Listen to Children Who've Just Been Separated from Their Parents at the Border," *ProPublica*, June 18, 2018. www. propublica.org/article/children-separated-from-parents-border-patrol-cbp-trump-immigration-policy

12 Ibid.

13 "A First-Hand Report of 'Inhumane Conditions" at a Migrant Children's Detention Facility," PBS News Hour, June 21, 2019. www.pbs.org/ newshour/show/a-firsthand-report-of-inhumane-conditions-at-a-migrant-childrens-detention-facility

14 Ibid.

15 Ibid.

16 Ibid.

17 Alex Ura, "State Leaders are Looking for Solutions After El Paso. Texas Latinos Say They Can Start by Changing the Words They Choose," *Texas Tribune*, August 22, 2019. www.texastribune.org/2019/08/22/what-hispanic-texans-want-texas-lawmakers-after-el-paso-shooting/

Four

The scene of the August 11, 2017 "Unite the Right" rally in Charlottesville, Virginia, exposed a sea of angry, racist white men—most of them carrying tiki torches, bedecked in pleated khakis and polo shirts. They chanted racist and anti-Semitic slogans in unison as they marched in the dark of night to protest the removal of a statue of Confederate General Robert E. Lee from Lee Park. In many ways, these angry faces are precisely what people imagine when thinking of the long history of violent racism in our nation. As Jenn M. Jackson says of this event, "Like many violent racial events in this country's past, history will record Charlottesville as a mixture of toxic masculinity and anti-black and anti-Semitic rage."[1] She recognizes that this kind of rage "paints white supremacy, and all of its trappings, as the domain of (white) men," but is quick to point out that this "couldn't be further from the truth."[2]

The role of white women in the sustainment and perpetuation of white supremacy is often understated in the popular imagination, but racist white women are an essential facet of that foundation. From slavery to Jim Crow, from the Ku Klux Klan to the Daughters of the Confederacy, and from 1619 to our present moment, white women have contributed to the continuation of white supremacy at the expense of the lives of Black men and women. Addressing the American public's shock and questioning how it was possible that 53% of white women voted for Donald Trump, a man who has made no attempt to mask his misogyny, Jackson says:

> But why are we still (seriously) asking that question now? Is it because we simply cannot fathom that many white women have a vested interest in white supremacy because it benefits them, too? Can we not envision a world where white women benefit from white privilege and power—whether they intend to or not? Are we so committed to our own logic and beliefs that we cannot believe the *actual* historical facts of the matter?[3]

We should not, in fact, be shocked that so many women disregarded Trump's sexism in their willingness to embrace his brand of racism. What we should do, and what this chapter seeks to do, is to interrogate this dynamic—one in which white women actively work to sustain white privilege and power, and yet so often are situated in the shadows of that racism. But if the racism that white women enact is often left unexamined, the racism that Black women endure is relegated to the background, too. This chapter brings both these issues to the fore.

When Sojourner Truth, in her famous 1851 speech, asks, "Ain't I a woman?," she underscores the estrangement of Black women when it comes to the fight for equality.[4] Such marginalization is ongoing, and Kimberlé Crenshaw has sharply attended to the oft-overlooked multifaceted oppression that women of color suffer. Crenshaw gestures at the need to consider "intragroup differences" when exploring issues of social justice for oppressed groups, and she focuses specifically on race and class for women who are victims of violence.[5] Indeed, we are much more familiar with names like Eric Garner and

Tamir Rice than we are with names like Natasha McKenna and Michelle Cusseaux, all of whom were unarmed Black individuals killed by police. All too often, women of color are ignored, even within the battle for women's rights. The belief in equality, then, is certainly not the same for everyone.

In the realm of Shakespeare, imaginings of powerful women are often laden with views of white superiority. By foregrounding Shakespeare's white heroines who successfully navigate, if not subvert, patriarchal expectations—characters like Portia in *The Merchant of Venice*, Rosalind in *As You Like It*, and Desdemona in *Othello*—this chapter interrogates how such ostensibly progressive views of women's power and resilience concurrently foreclose on the dignity for women of color and ignore the racist energies that define some white women. Portia exhibits explicit racism, Rosalind's elevated status is set against Celia's "browner" (4.3.93)[6] skin tone, and Desdemona expresses nostalgia for her former slave Barbary. If there are battles being fought and won where women's rights are concerned, those who are fighting these battles are also perpetuating anti-Blackness. The real-world implications of such views in our present moment are vital. Recent research attends to the disparities in access to healthcare for women of color, and findings reveal that Black women suffer death after childbirth at almost three times the rate of white women.[7] Three times! These grim statistics are indicative of social inequities across the board when it comes to Black women's healthcare and quality of life. Ultimately, the chapter considers how our exceptional nation, which was largely built on the backs of those like Sojourner Truth, unwaveringly neglects, degrades, and compromises the lives of so many Black and brown women.

Of the three Shakespeare characters I mentioned above, Rosalind might seem to many an unlikely choice to consider alongside issues of racism. Unlike *Merchant of Venice* and *Othello*, *As You Like It* is not labeled a "race play" by critics. As such, we don't necessarily consider it in terms of race, even if the play is indeed working to construct whiteness (this, of course, is applicable to all of Shakespeare's plays). For me, there are two moments in *As You Like It* that strike me as fundamentally significant where the elevation of whiteness is concerned, and both do much to bolster the view of Rosalind as an impressive woman in that play. The first comes when Rosalind and her cousin Celia decide to venture to the Forest of Arden in an effort to escape the tyranny of Celia's father, Duke Frederick. Rosalind makes the decision to cross-dress, seeing as she is "more than common tall" (1.3.122). Celia, in her own efforts to disguise herself as Aliena—with her chosen name clearly signaling her status as an "alien" or immigrant/stranger[8]— says she will dress "in poor and mean attire / And with a kind of umber smirch my face" (1.3.117–18). As Janna Segal says of this scene, "Rosalind will perform 'like a man'; she does not imagine herself capable of becoming one. Celia, however, will 'put [her]self' into her cross-class and cross-racial role, performing not just 'like' an alien, but rather, becoming Aliena."[9] To become Aliena, of course, is not possible. It is an elaborate act. Despite her prominent social standing, Celia diminishes herself by donning brownface. In many ways, the idea of embarking on the path of an immigrant to take refuge in a different space can only be imagined as an experience for those darker of skin. Without doubt, such a move imagines the immigrant as dark all the while allowing for the audience to believe that the actual whiteness beneath that exterior is superior, stable, and, not of little consequence, authentic. The audience knows that, ultimately, Celia will return to that prominent, white position.

The alignment of whiteness with a stable underpinning suggests a clear superiority and sense of belonging. I want to explore this, then, through the second moment of the play that strikes me as significant. When Orlando's brother Oliver arrives to explain to the two women (both still in disguise) that Orlando has been attacked by a lioness, he refers to Celia/ Aliena as "a woman low / And browner than her brother" (4.3.91–2). This reference serves to reify the view of Celia as lesser in stature both in terms of gender and skin color. When Rosalind hears the story of the lioness attacking Orlando and sees the bloody handkerchief that Oliver offers as proof, she proceeds to faint. When she comes to, Rosalind says, "I would I were at home" (4.3.170). Oliver ultimately asks, "You a man? You lack a man's heart" (4.3.174). Because of sexist assumptions, this moment serves to destabilize the power Rosalind holds in occupying the place of a man because she lacks the capacity—the "man's heart"—to encounter the violent reality of that space and to witness the bloody handkerchief. It's a facile understanding of gendered roles, where men are considered stronger and more courageous. But the scene isn't one that necessarily positions Rosalind as weak. Instead, one can read this moment as endearing because Rosalind ultimately exhibits the expected compassion for which the play seems to be pining. In her response, the audience is asked to recognize that she is deserving of a "home" and to feel empathy for the instability she feels in that moment. Rosalind deserves happiness. Visually, then, we see this, and we also see in the background the short stature and dark skin of Aliena as a reminder that some will never truly belong. As a dark woman in that scene, Aliena is powerless, uneventful, and easily ignored. She is the proverbial prop in the way so many Black servants served as diminutive props in Elizabethan portraiture.[10]

In not so subtle ways, the point of elevating the stature and whiteness of women in Shakespeare is to sustain the belief in white superiority. As Kim F. Hall argues of these poetic designs—or what she calls "poetics of color"—"whiteness is established as a valued goal."[11] Aliena, then, is ultimately able to get there by the play's end once her brown exterior is washed away and she reestablishes her authentic self as the white noblewoman Celia, who marries the white nobleman Oliver. It is the happy ending that we come to expect from the comedic genre. Once we focus on the stability and elevated stature of whiteness, we can ignore those darker of skin. They fade into nonexistence. So, what does such centering of whiteness, and in particular centering of white women, look like in our present moment?

In the opening anecdote of her stunning work, *The Erotic Life of Racism*, Sharon Patricia Holland describes "one of the defining moments" of her life.[12] As she explains, she was sitting in her car parked in a Safeway parking lot in Northern California with her friend's 15-year-old daughter, Danielle. They were listening to Tupac Shakur, who had recently died, and Danielle was sharing what his death meant to her and her friends. As Holland explains, "An older (but not elderly) woman with a grocery cart came to the driver's side of my car and asked me to move my vehicle so that she could unload her groceries. The tone of her voice assumed fruition—it was not only a request but a demand that would surely be met."[13] Seeing that there were no impediments on the other side of the woman's car, Holland told the woman that she would "gladly wait" in the car until the woman unloaded her groceries so she would have plenty of time to maneuver and so that Holland and Danielle could continue their "bonding" experience uninterrupted. Once the older white woman was done loading her groceries into her car, Holland and Danielle exited their own vehicle and Holland explains what happened next:

> As we passed the right rear bumper of her car, she said with mustered indignation, "And to think I marched for you!" I was stunned at first—when something like this happens to you, you see the whole event in slow motion. I recovered and decided that I had two options: to walk away without a word or to confront the accusation—to model for Danielle how to handle with a modicum of grace what would surely be part of the fabric of her life as a black woman in the United States. I turned to the woman and said, "You didn't march for me, you marched for yourself—and if you don't know that, I can't help you."[14]

Holland's opening story sheds light on the racist expectations that so many white people—even those who are seemingly woke—have about Black lives. As Holland says about that woman, "the civil rights struggle was not about freedom for us all, it was about acquiring a kind of purchase on black life."[15] The needs of that white woman will always come first, because whiteness is always centered. When those needs were not being met, that white woman tried to pull rank and remind the pair of Black women that they should be grateful to her. Lucky for Danielle, she was with a woman who knows what's what.

When Black women come into focus, though, as Holland does when she models confidence and self-respect for Danielle, then we can see the extent of the racism that seeks to define and diminish their value at every turn. Whiteness cannot be the valued goal—not in Shakespeare and not in our contemporary society. It is for this reason that, in Chapter 2, I gestured at the need to focus on the racism that a play like *The Merchant of Venice* holds. Much too often, critics focus on Portia's ability to inhabit, like Rosalind does, a masculine persona and brilliantly navigate masculine spaces. Indeed, as a literary critic, I am guilty of doing this in my first book. What is not highlighted enough is the sheer racism that underpins her character, her society, and that play. Where I have failed to do that before, I want to explore that here.

What *Merchant of Venice* offers us through Portia is a vivid picture of a racist white woman deeply invested in white supremacy. She derides foreigners, explicitly engages in anti-Blackness (as I explore in Chapter 2), and travels beyond the bounds of Belmont to aid powerful white men in sustaining white supremacy at the expense of Shylock's freedom. As Hall says of this play:

> Aliens must be either assimilated into the dominant culture (Shylock's and Jessica's conversions) and/or completely disempowered (Shylock's sentence). Their use as explanations for racial difference allows for the organization of property, kinship, and religion within an emerging national—and imperial—identity.[16]

That identity, she tells us, is established along gendered and racial lines. The play moves toward that end in its comedic—that is, its happy—resolution. I will reiterate here, *Merchant of Venice* is a play that should be taught and performed not in search of its call for humane treatment of Jews, but rather as an example of the monstrosity of white supremacy. If whiteness is centered, then we need to center the grotesque nature of those who view whiteness as superior. When Portia says to Shylock, "The quality of mercy is not strained" (4.1.190), she speaks from a position of privilege and power, even as a woman in a patriarchal society. We should not believe anything she offers us in the way of explaining mercy. It is Shylock's confidence in resisting that power that should catch our attention, as should the malignant mobilization to crush that confidence.

Confidence, when it comes from Black, Indigenous, and people of color, is often seen as a threat to the privileges that whiteness affords. The narrative about Black women's confidence, in particular, often maligns that confidence as anger, and that particular trope is often mobilized in an attempt to shatter said confidence. Serena Williams, for example, often found herself embroiled in controversy whenever she would call out injustices on the tennis court. She spoke up and spoke out, and that—like her Black body on a tennis court that had for so long been the domain of whites—made some people uneasy. Many a racist critic simply saw her as an angry Black woman in those moments of competition.

In her masterful work, *Citizen: An American Lyric*, Claudia Rankine considers the many incidents of racism that Williams suffered on the court and registers the weight of the injustices behind those experiences. Rankine examines one culminating moment when Williams said to a line judge, who erroneously called her for a foot fault during a pivotal moment of a Grand Slam match, "I swear to God I'm fucking going to take this fucking ball and shove it down your fucking throat."[17] Rankine makes it clear that replays and commentators, including John McEnroe, who had his fair share of emotional moments on the court, showed that there was not a foot fault. Still, the line judge called her for this foot fault and Williams was subsequently fined and put on probation by the Grand Slam Committee because of her response. Rankine writes of this:

> Perhaps the committee's decision is only about context, though context is not meaning. It is a public event being watched in homes across the world. In any case, it is difficult not to think that if Serena lost context by abandoning all rules of civility, it could be because her body, trapped in a racial imaginary, trapped in disbelief—code for being black in America—is being governed not by the tennis match she is participating in but by a collapsed relationship that had promised to play by the rules. Perhaps this is how racism feels no matter the context—randomly the rules everyone else gets to play by no longer apply to you, and to call this out by calling out "I swear to God!" is to be called insane, crass, crazy. Bad sportsmanship.[18]

But bad sportsmanship, when rules no longer apply to you, is precisely what needs to give. If the rules apply to some, but not to all, then there should be zero expectation for those at a disadvantage to stay quiet.

Indeed, when Williams argued a call with the Portuguese umpire, Carlos Ramos, years later at the 2018 U.S. Open championship, the scene reignited views regarding her needing to navigate when to stay quiet and when to speak up. Obviously, it was not the first time that Williams had challenged umpires or line judges on the court, as a pattern of injustices against her (and her vocal reactions to such injustices) was well in place. After this event, criticism poured in from every angle in regard to her "outburst" at the match. However, here I want to bypass that criticism to focus specifically on Williams' own view of the incident:

> It's the final of the US Open, and I'm competing to win my 24th Grand Slam against Naomi Osaka. It's the beginning of the second set, and the umpire thinks he spots my coach signaling me from the stands. He issues a violation—a warning. I approach him and emphatically state the truth: that I wasn't looking at my coach. "I don't cheat to win. I'd rather lose," I said. I walk back to the court and lose the next point. I smash my racket in frustration; he issues another violation and gives a point to my opponent. I feel passionately compelled to stand up for myself. I call him a thief; I again demand an apology. I tell him he is penalizing me for being a woman. He responds by issuing a third violation and takes a game from me. In the end, my opponent simply played better than me that day and ended up winning her first Grand Slam title. I could not have been happier for her. As for me, I felt defeated and disrespected by a sport that I love—one that I had dedicated my life to and that my family truly changed, not because we were welcomed, but because we wouldn't stop winning.[19]

In many ways, the act of slamming her racket in frustration is exactly the type of anger that fuels the belief that Black women cannot control their emotions, a belief at the heart of anti-Blackness. Williams did not stay poised. Williams cannot contain herself. Williams' anger is dangerous. Williams is dangerous. All of these perceptions of her exist solely because she is Black.

If we juxtapose Williams against an array of white men and women who have shown emotion on the court, we see that the only difference is her Blackness. I am struck by Williams explicitly saying she felt disrespected not just by Ramos, but by the very sport she loved—a sport, she makes clear, that did not welcome her but that *had* to accept her because she kept winning. As she says later in her essay,

> I've been called every name in the book. I've been shamed because of my body shape. I've been paid unequally because of my sex. I've been penalized a game in the final of a major because I expressed my opinion or grunted too loudly. I've been blatantly cheated against to the point where the Hawk-Eye rules were introduced so that something like that would not happen again. And these are only the things that are seen by the public. In short, it's never been easy. But then I think of the next girl who is going to come along who looks like me, and I hope, "Maybe, just maybe, my voice will help her."[20]

The particular notion that her voice, her confidence, might serve as a model of emulation for a young, Black girl waiting in the wings is akin to the anecdote Holland shared where she, too, stood up against racist views of the way she should behave so that her friend's 15-year old daughter could bear witness to such self-confidence. But like the older white woman in the Safeway parking lot, Ramos or the sport of tennis has never apologized to Williams. They feel they are the victims of her Black rage, and they feel entitled to keep such Black women in their place.

This dynamic of white entitlement, of course, is also applicable to *Othello*, which I explored in my opening chapter. I want to return here to *Othello* so as to consider a bit more closely the role of Desdemona within that play, and not through the brilliant imaginings of Toni Morrison's *Desdemona* (though certainly influenced by that work). Like Portia and Rosalind, Desdemona is able to subvert patriarchal expectations within her own society. When the play opens, we learn she has eloped with Othello, a Black man, so she very explicitly defies expectations both by circumventing her father's approval and by entering into an interracial marriage. What critics quite often focus on is the racialized body of Othello, and what his Blackness means when we consider the role of Desdemona in the play. However, what I want to consider is the racialized body of Desdemona.

There are various moments in *Othello* where fairness is imagined as both beautiful and virtuous. Desdemona's fairness, then, is sometimes emphasized to define her. For his part, Othello calls her "fair paper" (4.2.82) and later describes her skin as whiter "than snow" (5.2.4). This is all to say, the text itself makes her whiteness visible to us. If Othello's Blackness is being defined, so is Desdemona's whiteness. As such, I want to consider—as many critics have done when it comes to the connection between Othello's skin color and the loss of his stature and self-worth—how Desdemona navigates her whiteness when she no longer occupies an unchallenged privileged position. That is, I want to scrutinize the moment that inspired Toni Morrison to write *Desdemona*—when Desdemona evokes her former "maid" (i.e. slave) Barbary in this play.

Desdemona's reference to Barbary comes after Othello strikes her in public and later privately accuses her of being promiscuous. Othello says to Desdemona, "Was this fair paper, this most goodly book, / Made to write 'whore' upon? What committed? / Committed? O though public commoner" (4.2.82–4). Later he mocks her protestations at being accused of infidelity and says to her, "I cry you mercy, then. / I took you for that cunning whore of Venice / That married with Othello" (4.2.103–5). Those actions, in themselves, clearly traumatize Desdemona. However, we should also note that in the midst of those acts, Othello is also dismissed from his post at Cyprus, and thus he must leave. As Iago makes clear, "He goes into Mauritania and takes away with him the fair Desdemona" (4.2.256–7). To this point, Desdemona has lived among her own in Venice, and even in her short stay at Cyprus, she is surrounded by Venetians. With her fair skin, Desdemona will then be the stranger in Mauritania.

How much of this does Desdemona realize at that moment in the play. Obviously, it is unclear, but her seeming nostalgia for childhood is, I think, indicative of an understanding that she is losing standing and privilege because her husband, darker of skin, no longer holds her on a pedestal. But while her power seems to fade, the perceived superiority of her whiteness remains. She says of her childhood:

> My mother had a maid called Barbary.
> She was in love, and he she loved proved mad
> And did forsake her. She had a song of willow,
> And old thing 'twas, but it expressed her fortune,
> And she died singing it. That song tonight
> Will not go from my mind. I have much to do,
> But to go hang my head all at one side
> And sing it like poor Barbary.
>
> (4.3.28–35)

While on the surface, she is simply expressing a connection to her former "maid" because, like Barbary, Desdemona has a love who is proving mad. However, there might be more at work here. Peter Erickson offers us a more compelling take on this scene. He writes: "The specific legacy of slavery that she receives through her mother also comes into play here because the hierarchical image of her white power over the black maid provides an easy replacement for the unstable, uncontrollable relationship with the black Othello."[21] It is a moment where Desdemona must resituate herself, because she is on unstable ground with her Black husband. Recalling her former slave allows her to do that along racialized lines.

What I find interesting is that Desdemona has, in her presence, Emilia, who is her attendant. I certainly do not mean to suggest here that Emilia's role is similar to that of Barbary, but where her social status is concerned, Desdemona is still in a privileged position. Emilia's own whiteness, though, seems to delimit how Desdemona feels about herself. Erickson goes on to write about the role of Barbary in this scene:

As her perception of Othello moves from his being the good African to the possibly bad African, Desdemona's memory of Barbary is suddenly brought forth as the new good African who fills the vacuum left by Othello. Although she is innocent of the infidelity of which the deluded Othello accuses her, Desdemona's gesture of claiming her mother's black maid seems less so. Having lost her black husband, she turns for a dependable and safe alternative to a conveniently available black woman of lower social status from her childhood. The black maid is also conveniently dead: she can neither talk back nor offer resistance, and so her meaning is completely malleable to

> Desdemona's needs. Through this substitution, Desdemona
> finds a servant who can serve as a sympathetic vehicle for
> expressing her own feelings ... In an act of white entitlement,
> Desdemona adopts and channels the elegiac appeal of the
> maid's plaintive melancholy.[22]

Desdemona's own racialized body, then, must be defined along lines of superiority, even as her lived experiences in that moment register oppression. This is the convenient illusion surrounding Black lives—they exist for the sole purpose of centering and elevating whiteness. We cannot ignore this facet of Desdemona simply because she seems "progressive" enough to enter into a marriage with a Black man. That, to borrow from Holland, does not give her the right to feel that she has acquired "a kind of purchase on Black life."

The deployment of the conveniently dead and silent Barbary to highlight Desdemona's suffering not only privileges whiteness but altogether undermines the absent character. Barbary's sadness matters only because it registers Desdemona's sadness, and is not in and of itself important. Barbary is not in and of herself important. This is the brilliance of Toni Morrison restoring a voice of resistance and giving Barbary a name. So often, as Imtiaz Habib's vital work has shown, Black people in Shakespeare's England were nameless and invisible.[23] But this, for me, is also what is so hard-hitting about these cross-historical perspectives, as erasure and silencing of Black women persist to our present moment. We need to listen and recognize that the diminishment of their value through systems of white supremacy—explicit and implicit in our current time—is quite often a matter of life and death.

Most of us, I hope, are aware of the disparities in healthcare when it comes to Black versus white women. The statistics for pregnancy-related deaths for Black women are particularly sobering. According to the Centers for Disease Control and Prevention (CDC), Black, American Indian, and Alaska Native women are "two to three times more likely to die from pregnancy-related causes than white women."[24] As the CDC notes, "Most pregnancy related deaths are preventable. Racial and ethnic disparities in pregnancy-related deaths have persisted over time."[25] The persistence of these disparities is telling. If these deaths are preventable, why are they not being prevented? Health professionals have this information, and yet clearly there is no investment in widespread reform to address these disparities. This is an epidemic, and yet little attention is being paid likely because Black and Indigenous women are seen as expendable, even within a system that is meant to save lives.

In an article that thoroughly outlines the various factors at work in healthcare disparities across the board for Black women, Erika Stallings is unafraid to consider the role of racial bias in medical care. Stallings asks us to "consider that the mortality rate for babies born to black women with a doctorate or professional degree is higher than the rate for babies born to white women who never finished high school. A picture begins to emerge of forces at once bigger, deeper, and more insidious at play."[26] The role of racism, Stallings tells us, is a major factor in diminished health and healthcare for Black women. And although medical studies prove this, little has been done to change the system. As long as racism persists, disparities will follow. Stallings writes:

> That's the reality of being a black woman dealing with this country's healthcare system. Too often, we have to go an extra mile—many extra miles—just to ensure we get the

baseline level of treatment to which everyone is entitled. And
all the while, we have to ask ourselves: *Was I mistreated
because of my race?*[27]

Many healthcare workers might answer, "of course not," to
that question, but so often bias is clearly in place, and Stallings
demonstrates this with medical study after medical study, as
well as anecdote after anecdote.

To be a Black woman in this nation often means to be
ignored, silenced, and put in a state of precariousness because
of the color of your skin. As Stallings says, "just as a house
continually battered by storms will eventually list, sag, and
crumble, the health of black people in America is corroded by
the relentless assaults of racism."[28] This is, indeed, the insidious
nature of a society that sometimes looks at racism, denounces
it, and yet does absolutely nothing to change structures of
white supremacy, because so long as the structure continues
to privilege whiteness, for so many, there is little to care about
beyond that. This is why we should not be surprised that so
many white women voted for Trump. But what so many of
these white women need to recognize is that the disparagement and disregard for Black lives does not improve the situation for white women and, of more importance, reforms
that address racial inequities will not result in less for white
women. Such reforms would simply serve as a corrective so
that every single patient gets the adequate healthcare they
deserve. For many, even that is too big of an ask.

The weight of this for Black women is, I think, why we
need to interrogate the striking disparities when it comes to
womanhood and white supremacy. In her breathtaking play,
Harlem Duet, Djanet Sears thoughtfully interrogates such disparities by appropriating Shakespeare's *Othello* to consider the

effects of racism on a Black woman.[29] Set in three different periods—the U.S. South in 1860s, Harlem in 1928, and the present day—*Harlem Duet* imagines Othello in love with Billie, a Black woman, prior to and during his relationship with Desdemona. Near the end of the first act, Billie contemplates the tragic history of those who have come in contact with the famed handkerchief as a way to articulate the tragic history of so many Black people in this nation. Ultimately, she considers the privileged racism of white women:

> While Susan Smith... She blamed some imaginary Black man for the murder of her two boys and that's why authorities didn't suspect her for nearly two weeks. Stopping every Black man with a burgundy sedan from Union, South Carolina, to the Oranges of New Jersey. And you're still wondering what made her do it. What was she going through to make her feel that this was her only way out. Yet I'll be discarded as some kind of unconscionable bitter shadow, or something. Ain't I a woman? This is my face you take for night—the biggest shadow in the world.
>
> (1.10)[30]

For Billie, the understanding that even the most monstrous of white women like Susan Smith are afforded serves to overshadow and diminish her worth—her very presence in this world—because the truth is that Black women are not afforded the same understanding.

Sure, we can be outraged by the bravado of racist white men in khakis carrying tiki torches, but in reality we need to look deeper, examine more closely, and see that these racist structures run incredibly deep and are heartbreakingly damaging—especially for women of color. As Kimberlé

Crenshaw says of the multifaceted forms of racism that Black men and women face in our nation, "In this horror story, the terror is in recognizing that our flight from one monster leaves us prey to another. If these monsters are not confronted, there will always be another."[31] We need to look closely at those who are complicit in this monstrosity, and we need to dig deep to consider what we are doing to confront it.

NOTES

1 Jenn M. Jackson, "Women Have Always Been a Part of White Supremacy," *Teen Vogue*, August 20, 2017. https://jennmjackson.com/2017/08/20/women-have-always-been-a-part-of-white-supremacy/

2 Ibid.

3 Ibid.

4 I am aware that the veracity of Sojourner Truth making this statement is in dispute, and my investment in this statement has more to do with its influence on the way we consider the inclusion/exclusion of Black women in the women's rights movement. Indeed, this chapter's title derives from Djanet Sears' keen use of this phrase in her work (see below). For more on the controversy surrounding Sojourner Truth's speech, see, Rachel Chang, "Sojourner Truth's 'Ain't I a Woman' Speech May Not Have Contained That Famous Phrase," *Biography*, February 13, 2020. www.biography.com/news/sojourner-truth-aint-i-a-woman-speech

5 Kimberlé Crenshaw, "Mapping the Margins: Intersectionality, Identity Politics, and Violence Against Women of Color," *Stanford Law Review* 43.6 (1991), 1242.

6 William Shakespeare, *As You Like It*, ed. Barbara Mowat and Paul Werstine (New York: Folger Shakespeare Library, 1997).

7 Nina Martin, "Black Mothers Keep Dying After Giving Birth. Shalon Irving's Story Explains Why," *NPR.org*, December 7, 2017. www.npr.org/2017/12/07/568948782/black-mothers-keep-dying-after-giving-birth-shalon-irvings-story-explains-why

8 For more on labels used to identify foreigners, see the introduction to *Shakespeare and Immigration*, ed. Ruben Espinosa and David Ruiter (New York: Routledge, 2014).

9 Janna Segal, "'And browner than her brother': 'Misprized' Celia's Racial Identity and Transversality in *As You Like It*." *Shakespeare* 4.1 (2008), 8.

10 See, for example, Peter Erickson, "Invisibility Speaks: Servants and Portraiture in Early Modern Visual Culture," *The Journal for Early Modern Cultural Studies* 9.1, 2009.

11 Kim F. Hall, *Things of Darkness: Economies of Race and Gender in Early Modern England* (Ithaca, NY: Cornell UP, 1995), 66.

12 Sharon Patricia Holland, *The Erotic Life of Racism* (Durham, NC: Duke UP, 2012), 2.

13 Ibid., 1.

14 Ibid., 2.

15 Ibid., 2.

16 Kim F. Hall, "Guess Who's Coming to Dinner? Colonization and Miscegenation in *The Merchant of Venice*," *Renaissance Drama* 23: 101–2.

17 Claudia Rankine, *Citizen: An American Lyric* (Minneapolis, MN: Graywolf Press, 2014), 29.

18 Ibid., 30

19 Serena Williams, "Serena Poses Unretouched for Harper's Bazaar," *Harper's Bazaar*, July 9, 2019. www.harpersbazaar.com/culture/features/a28209579/serena-williams-us-open-2018-essay/

20 Ibid.

21 Peter Erickson, "Race Words in *Othello*," *Shakespeare and Immigration*, ed. Ruben Espinosa and David Ruiter (Burlington, VT: Ashgate, 2014), 166.

22 Ibid., 166.

23 See Imtiaz Habib, *Black Lives in the English Archives, 1500–1677: Imprints of the Invisible* (New York: Routledge, 2007).

24 "Racial and Ethnic Disparities Continue in Pregnancy-Related Deaths," Centers for Disease Control and Prevention, September 5, 2019. www.cdc.gov/media/releases/2019/p0905-racial-ethnic-disparities-pregnancy-deaths.html

25 Ibid.

26 Erika Stallings, "This is How the American Healthcare System Is Failing Black Women," *The Oprah Magazine*, August 1, 2018. www.oprahmag.com/life/health/a23100351/racial-bias-in-healthcare-black-women/

27 Ibid.

28 Ibid.

29 For a keen reading of this play with sustained attention to its exploration of cycles of oppression, see Nedda Medizadeh, "Othello in Harlem: Transforming the Theater in Djanet Sears's *Harlem Duet*," *Journal of American Studies* 54.1 (2020).

30 Djanet Sears, *Harlem Duet* (Winnipeg: Scirocco Drama, 1997), 75.

31 Kimberlé Williams Crenshaw, "The Unmattering of Black Lives," *The New Republic*, May 21, 2020. https://newrepublic.com/article/157769/unmattering-black-lives

Five

When the eponymous hero of *Henry V* rallies his soldiers around the idea of a shared brotherhood that crosses the borders of cultural identity and social hierarchies, he lies to them. In the aftermath of Henry's St. Crispin's Day speech and the famous victory at Agincourt, there is no true brotherhood between the English, Scots, Irish, or Welsh, just as there is no true brotherhood between the king and his lowly subjects. Division remains. Case in point: When Henry receives the death count for the French and English, he takes time to name the men of nobility and gentry who died—15 from France, and four from England—and then says of the English dead, "None else of name, and all of other men / But five and twenty" (4.8.109–10). Twenty-five of his "brothers" remain nameless because they are expendable in his eyes. Division remains. Case in point: after the victory, the Welshman Fluellen challenges the English soldier/thief Pistol because the latter mocked Fluellen's Welsh identity and customs, and in particular Fluellen's act of wearing a leek in his hat to honor the patron saint of Wales, Saint David. Rather than swallow his pride, Fluellen instead chooses to confront Pistol about this at a more appropriate moment. When Fluellen finally addresses Pistol, he beats him, berates him, and force feeds him a leek. As Fluellen departs, the Englishman Gower says to Pistol, "You thought because he could not speak English in the native garb, he could not therefore handle an English cudgel. You find it otherwise, and henceforth let a Welsh correction teach you a good English condition" (5.2.79–83). So much for "we band of brothers" (4.3.62).

What these post-war moments in *Henry V* reveal is that social hierarchies, inequitable structures of power, and ethnocentrism all remain in place for the English. If *Henry V* is fostering a sense of English nationalism, it is also illustrating that such an organization of community, by nature, rejects inclusivity. Some are deemed important while others remain nameless. Pistol is hardly superior to Fluellen as a soldier or in any other noticeable capacity, and yet his ethnocentrism and bravado pave the way for him to elevate Englishness by ridiculing Fluellen's Welsh cultural traditions. Indeed, the play itself underscores Fluellen's inexact command of the English language, and this undoubtedly allows his audience to laugh at him, too. To "jest at strangers, because they speak not English so well as we do," Shakespeare's contemporary Sir Philip Sidney argues, goes "against the law of hospitality."[1] But, as I argue in Chapter 2, that is precisely the point in *Henry V*—England's greatness must be set against neighbors who are deemed "of baser quality" (1.1.65).

Perhaps the lesson we should think through is the one that Fluellen's forceful resistance offers to us. Fluellen hardly sees Pistol, or the English for that matter, as superior in any recognizable way, and he is explicit about the pride he feels about his Welsh identity. Indeed, at the very moment Henry is trying to memorialize the English victory at Agincourt by connecting it to the celebration of St. Crispin's Day, Fluellen uses the opportunity to centralize the significance of the Welsh: "Your grandfather of famous memory, an 't please your Majesty, and your great-uncle Edward the Plack Prince of Wales, as I have read in the chronicles, fought a most prave pattle here in France." Henry responds, "They did, Fluellen" (4.7.97–101). Fluellen then says:

> Your Majesty says very true. If your Majesties is remembered of it, the Welshmen did good service in a garden where leeks did grow, wearing leeks in their Monmouth caps, which, your Majesty know, to this hour is an honorable badge of the service. And I do believe your Majesty takes no scorn to wear the leek upon Saint Tavy's day.
>
> (4.7.102–8)

This seemingly insignificant digression on the part of Fluellen is actually quite important, because whether he means to or not, Fluellen's recollection of Welsh service on French soil and the memorialization of that battle via the wearing of a leek on Saint David's day make both Henry and the English audience aware that their neighbors of baser quality have a deep history with long-established cultural traditions. If Henry is trying to memorialize St. Crispin's Day, Fluellen is there to remind him to get in line.

The firm resolve to push back against those who seek to diminish one's value is vital, and yet, Fluellen going it alone is not the answer. There needs to be, ironically enough, the kind of shared community that the elitist Henry inspires in *Henry V*. In many ways, *Henry V* offers its audience, both then and now, an opportunity to scrutinize early perceptions of English ethnocentrism, but it also lends itself to seeing how jingoism and aspirations for empire are bolstered against those deemed less powerful and less alike. In our present moment, and with the racism of white supremacy in mind, views of U.S. nationalism are no less dangerous. As the previous chapters have demonstrated, Black and brown individuals share quite a bit when it comes to confronting structures of white supremacy and nationalistic sentiments based on exclusion, and as such, sustained attention to solidarity among Black and brown people against white supremacy is of tantamount importance.

In varied ways, as the previous chapters have argued, Shakespeare's work often gestures at our ethical responsibilities to each other in both implicit and explicit ways—Shylock's call for us to consider his humanity, Hamlet's understanding of the value of hospitality, and Sir Thomas More's forceful investment in inspiring empathy for immigrants all come to mind. To follow Shakespeare along these lines is to recognize our obligations when it comes to fostering equity and inclusion without provision. The key begins with forging Black-brown solidarity so as to recognize in the individuals beyond our own borders (corporeal, political, and geographical) the potential for a concentrated effort to locate liberation from colonial structures that continue to define and delimit the value of so many.

Theorizing hybridity as an "imaginative rather than an embodied or corporeal example of race mixture," John Márquez suggests that such an approach stands to offer us "a model and praxis of solidarity that unsettles and destabilizes the identitarian silos and colonial politics of recognition that are necessitated by neoliberal multiculturalism."[2] In other words, instead of focusing on the divergence between Black and brown, we need to scrutinize the structures that rely on said divergence. Márquez considers the apprehension some Black leaders feel when it comes to aligning their antiracist activist efforts with similar Latinx efforts because it diminishes attention to the specific struggles surrounding anti-Blackness, and he writes:

This partitioning of antiblack racism away from a
more diverse conversation regarding white supremacy
represents, to some extent, a politically conservative ethic
that is cloaked by a progressive and antiracist veneer,
a kind of post-civil rights and liberal bipolarism that is
encouraged by the protocols of neoliberal multiculturalism
and the persistent pressure for groups to accentuate all
that is unique about their plight and to secure spaces
and resources belatedly granted them by lamenting or
sympathetic whites. There are, however, critical elements
to that position that deserve to be analyzed... To be sure,
African Americans have experienced racism in unique and
uniquely profound ways and largely as the result of
chattel slavery, Jim Crow, and the advent of the prison
industrial complex. In addition antiblack racism is not
exclusive to white subjectivities and is evident across
Latino/a, Asian American, Arab American and Native
American communities.[3]

Márquez's attention to the reach of anti-Black racism is
important for us to consider, because the fact that racism and
xenophobia cross color lines and borders means that it is often
difficult to carve a path to solidarity when one is unwilling
to recognize in the oppression of others one's own subjugation under, and negotiation of, colonial politics. Still, it seems
possible to recognize, as Márquez does, both the "uniquely
profound" experiences of anti-Blackness *and* the opportunity for Black and brown individuals to come together and
challenge the white supremacy that undergirds that racism.
While experiences for Blacks and Latinxs certainly differ in a
multitude of ways, Márquez argues, they are "bound together
in their shared experience of expendability."[4] This chapter

considers the shared experience of expendability for Black and brown people to underscore how, through the hybridity that Márquez imagines, such a praxis of solidarity could unsettle the manifold dynamics that result in oppression of, and violence against, people of color.

My intent, as I mention in the introduction to this book, is not to conflate histories and experiences for Black and brown individuals, but rather to recognize the value of shared efforts for these groups to challenge structures of white supremacy that situate them in precarious states of existence. The pressure on people of color to approximate whiteness is substantial, if only because the long history of colonialism and anti-Blackness has imagined those dark of skin as inherently inferior. But efforts to approximate whiteness, of course, are futile and often serve only to underscore the divide between Black and brown, and the desire of the latter to move away from the former. However, as Márquez writes:

> These dedicated, troubling, and sustained attempts by Latinos/as at whitening and assimilation have never really ... resulted in much of a general socioeconomic benefit for them ... In fact Latinidad as an ethnoracial signifier of both deficiency and menace has been produced and reproduced in stark opposition to discourses regarding U.S. citizenship, a form of "racialization" that is exacerbated by the U.S.-Mexico border to an insidiously fatal extent and that perpetuates the uninterrupted imperilment of Latino/a life.[5]

Márquez's point here is worth lingering over, as he gestures at the inefficacy of Latinxs trying to approximate whiteness while concurrently recognizing that attitudes about perceived deficits surrounding Latinxs define views of their (un) belonging in America. When whiteness is upheld as something to which those who are not white should aspire, then the viciousness of white supremacy has teeth. Always, there is failure on that front for Latinxs, and always views of their value are rooted in their perceived illegitimacy. This understanding of Latinxs as not quite American is certainly applicable to Blacks in the United States as well. The need to push back against such ideals and delineations of worth is, from where I stand, of the utmost importance. Don't take my word for it, though.

Discussing the reluctance for Black and Latinx communities to come together in solidarity against similar systems of oppression, Angela Davis is unequivocal about the need to value such a possibility. She says:

> One of the things that we need to remember is that the victories that have been won in the struggle for black freedom never would have been possible if only black people were the ones who were active in those struggles. ... I know my case would not have been won, as it was, had not it been for the activism of the Chicano community in San Jose when I was tried on charges of ... conspiracy. In San Jose, there was a very minuscule black community there at that time. And it was in the Chicano community that the major organizing took place. I don't understand how people can assume that its possible for each racialized ethnic group to go it alone.[6]

Again, if we recognize that the struggle is against systems of white supremacy, then Black-brown solidarity should be a given. In the case of Angela Davis, clearly the San Jose Chicanx community rallied behind somebody they admired because they understood that she was unafraid to challenge racist structures and white supremacy. They felt compelled to lend their support to her because these racist structures affected them, too. Similarly, Davis feels compelled to support Latinxs struggling against the very same system of oppression. Black-brown solidarity like this is vital. This is not to say, though, that through the solidarity between Black and brown we ought to eschew white allyship—we should not. As Derrick Bell says about critical race theorists, "Those … who are white are usually cognizant of and committed to the overthrow of their own racial privilege."[7] But it is tantamount that the struggle begins by forging a sense of community among those who are Black and brown and who are the primary targets of white supremacy, because when that struggle is solitary, those of us dark of skin run the risk of becoming Calibans.

I invoke Caliban here because I think *The Tempest* offers an interesting snapshot into the way systems of white supremacy work. The underlying belief behind white supremacy deems that those born white are superior to all others, and that defending that superiority should be accomplished at all costs. The advantageous position they hold is imagined as their birthright. The structures that define the social hierarchies of both *The Tempest* and Shakespeare's England operate along similar lines, as people in those worlds are born into specific social hierarchies that define their value. Moreover, the belief in white supremacy is also a significant facet of the play.

Before I arrive at the play's attention to white supremacy, though, I want to draw attention to the importance of the play's willingness to underscore uneven social structures. Take, for example, the opening moments of *The Tempest*, when the Boatswain is attempting to keep the ship afloat in the storm but is being questioned by Alonso, the King of Naples, and his councilor Gonzalo. Clearly irritated by their presence and interference, the Boatswain asks them to leave. As Gonzalo reluctantly begins to depart, he says to the Boatswain, "Good, yet remember whom thou hast aboard" (1.1.20)[8] He is directly referencing the King of Naples here, and the expectation is that the Boatswain should do his best to save Alonso. The Boatswain, though, retorts:

> None that I more love than myself. You are a councillor; if you can comment these elements to silence, and work the peace of the present, we will not hand a rope more. Use your authority. If you cannot, give thanks you have lived so long and make yourself ready in your cabin for the mischance of the hour, if it so hap.
>
> (1.1.21–7)

This is a moment of impressive resistance, as the Boatswain speaks aloud in the presence of the king's councilor his belief that it is his own life that he values most. Moreover, he points directly to the inefficacy of Gonzalo's authority in that moment. Social hierarchies cease to matter here.

Still, we would be hard pressed to believe that the Boatswain alone can dismantle such structures of power. As Gonzalo says in response to the Boatswain, "I have great comfort from this fellow. Methinks he hath no drowning mark upon him. His complexion is perfect gallows" (1.1.29–31). In other words, should they survive, Gonzalo is already preparing to have the Boatswain hanged for his insolence. The response, of course, is meant to be comedic, but the use of the gallows in the history of England reflects the more sobering reality of the power

Shakespeare on the Shades of Racism

structures that were in place. Monarchy demands respect for those above. For those below? Well, like the Boatswain, one must look out for oneself.

That attention to systems of power where the superiority of the monarch and nobility is upheld by the many, while the suffering of those in states or oppression is experienced in isolation is telling. Indeed, we can neatly divide the play into those who hold political power and those who do not. First, we have Alonso, Gonzalo, and the noblemen and courtiers who accompany them—Antonio, Sebastian, Adrian, and Francisco. Also in that first group are Prospero, the former Duke of Milan, Miranda, his daughter, and Ferdinand, Alonso's son. All the aforementioned rank relatively high in the social hierarchy even if, on the island, that hierarchy can be only imagined. In the group that holds no political power we have the servant Trinculo, the butler Stephano, the Boatswain and other shipmen, and Caliban. Ariel is a spirit with supernatural powers, but still under the control of Prospero. One sees, then, the proverbial haves and the have nots—again, as forged in the world outside of that island (except for Ariel, of course, who is otherworldly). When the have nots interact, though, further divisions arise. Trinculo and Stephano are quick to bring Caliban into submission and have him as their would-be servant. Indeed, shortly after Caliban meets these men and drinks from the wine, he says to Stephano, "I'll show thee every fertile inch o' th' island, and I will kiss thy foot. I prithee, be my god" (2.2.154–5). Because Caliban is so often seen as a representation of the Black or Indigenous other in Shakespeare's world, such delineations matter.

Some would have us believe that *The Tempest* has nothing to do with colonialism or that particular legacy. Indeed, Harold

Bloom lambasts any reader who sees Caliban as anything beyond a "half-human creature" who stands to represent an "African-Caribbean heroic Freedom fighter."[9] According to Bloom, "anyone who arrives at that view is simply not interested in reading the play at all."[10] What Bloom, situated in his own privileged, white, male position, likely means is that anyone who does not see the play in the way he sees it is not worth acknowledging. And yet by suggesting that we should not acknowledge it, he does acknowledge it because the issue of race is clearly a prominent theme in *The Tempest*. For Bloom, the issue of race isn't worth discussing, and thus he straightforwardly says that we should dismiss it. I can't and I don't. But please don't chalk that up to my dark skin and perceived outsider status as a Chicano Shakespearean—chalk it up to the fact that I'm a disciplined scholar who is in fact not only interested but also invested in reading the play with zero fear of confronting its racist paradigms. Unlike Bloom, I have no white privilege to protect.

It seems irresponsible to me for someone like Bloom to evade the play's clear attention to the energies of colonialism in the way it situates Caliban. If, as Bloom suggests, Caliban is less than human, it is because so many white men and women in that period imagined those darker of skin as less than human. Indeed, the arguments Trinculo puts forward would suggest as much. When Trinculo first sees Caliban, he says:

> What have we here? A man or a fish? Dead or alive? A fish, he smells like a fish—a very ancient and fishlike smell, a kind of not-of-the-newest poor-John. A strange fish. Were I in England now, as once I was, and had but this fish painted, not a holiday fool there but would give a piece of silver. There would this monster make a man. Any strange beast there

makes a man. When they will not give a doit to relieve a
lame beggar, they will lay out ten to see a dead Indian.

(2.2.26–33)

Trinculo imagines putting Caliban on display and says of the
English (and not his own Neapolitans) that they are eager to
behold "a dead Indian." The project of colonization demands
that the colonizer see the colonized as subhuman so that the
subjugation of human beings is justifiable in their eyes. But
even Trinculo can see through the greed of such an enterprise.
In one single line, he speaks to the inhumanity of the English
who are unwilling to help the poor, but willing to pay to see
those that the colonizers captured and, in the process, support
the colonizing enterprise.

Later in the play Trinculo is taken by Caliban's willingness
to serve Stephano and says, "A most scurvy monster. I could
find it in my heart to beat him" (2.2.161–2). While this
moment in the play is clearly meant to be comedic, the sinister undertones of such a sentiment reveal to us the grotesque
nature of enslavement and/or the genocide enacted on the
Indigenous population of the Americas. We must remember
that Caliban is eager to serve Stephano and Trinculo because
he wants to escape the abuse he has endured under Prospero,
who has enslaved him. Early on Prospero says to Caliban,
"Thou most lying slave, / Whom stripes may move, not
kindness" (1.2.413). The stripes in question, of course, refer
to those Caliban receives when he is whipped. Anyone who
arrives at the view that Trinculo's statement and Prospero's
warning and threat to whip Caliban do not reflect the realities
of racism is not interested in reading the play at all.

The truth, of course, is that many do not want to acknowledge racism in the play or in our world because it means they

have to acknowledge what they gain or maintain through their complicity in structures that privilege whiteness. In so many ways, it is easy to see the eagerness of Trinculo and Stephano to exploit someone they deem below them because, in no uncertain terms, they have been exploited, too. Yet this is not at all the shared experience of expendability that Márquez puts forward. This is a moment where two white men find an opportunity to exploit someone deemed lesser than not because of his social status but because of his physical attributes. For this reader, this is a remarkable moment that points to the play's attention to white supremacy.

To get to the heart of the racism that structures *The Tempest*, however, we need to look intently at those who have the power to sustain systems of white supremacy. We should, then, go straight to the top of that hierarchy. As much as Alonso exists as a character who seems to garner sympathy because he believes his son, Ferdinand, drowned in the tempest, the racism that surrounds him and his rationale, from where I stand, ought to be underscored any time we encounter this play. The Boatswain gives us the roadmap at the onset, and it is up to audiences to see that systems that imagine a particular birthright need to be eradicated. As Alonso and the other noblemen walk about the island on which they're stranded, Gonzalo attempts to distract Alonso with conversation by mentioning how odd it is that their clothes still look as fresh as when they departed Africa, when Alonso's daughter, Claribel, married the King of Tunis. Alonso ignores Gonzalo for some time, but ultimately lashes out:

> You cram these words into mine ears against
> The stomach of my sense. Would I had never

Married my daughter there, for coming thence
My son is lost, and, in my rate, she too,
Who is so far from Italy removed
I ne'er again shall see her.

(2.1.112–17)

On the surface, it is the geographical distance from his
daughter that adds to the grief at the belief his son has died.
Francisco tries to give him hope that Ferdinand might still
live, but Sebastian, Alonso's brother, is having none of it. He
says to Alonso about Ferdinand's presumed death:

Sir, you may thank yourself for this great loss,
That would not bless our Europe with our daughter,
But rather lose her to an African,
Where she at least is banished from your eye,
Who hath cause to wet the grief on 't.

(2.1.131–5)

Sebastian blames Alonso for the position they are in because
he agreed to marry Claribel to the King of Tunis, an African,
and thus they were forced to travel by sea and thus meet the
horrific tempest. The not so subtle subtext here is the racism
that informs Sebastian's view. He suggests that, had Claribel
been married to a European man, then they would not be
in this position. We can, perhaps, consider arguments that
focus on the levels of precarity for land travel as opposed to
sea travel, but we shouldn't. Sebastian is clear when he says
Alonso should have blessed "our" Europe with "our" daughter
Claribel, and thus believes whiteness belongs to them. But,
again, don't take my word for it.

Even though Alonso asks his brother to stop chastising him, Sebastian continues in expressing his disdain regarding the interracial marriage of his niece. Sebastian says:

> You were kneeled to and importuned otherwise
> By all of us, and the fair soul herself
> Weighed between loathness and obedience at
> Which end o' th' beam should bow.

(2.1.137–40)

Again, the geographical distance is not the issue. Indeed, the distance between Naples and Tunis is less than the distance between Naples and any European country north of Italy.[11] The issue here is the deep desire by Sebastian and many of others in Naples to keep the "fair" (i.e. white) Claribel from marrying an African. Claribel's own "loathness" for entering this marriage is also mentioned. It is obedience and obedience alone that led to that marriage, and the current situation in which they find themselves is a direct result of that decision. The danger of Blackness here is explicitly put forward. To put it more bluntly, all those white men think that the reason for their misfortune is because of a Black man.

I am attuned to the racism here because, again, I am interested in reading the play, but I'm also attuned to the source of that racism. This is to say, I'm not fooled nor roped into the desire to consider the way the King of Tunis factors into this narrative. It is clear to me he is being presented as the proverbial boogeyman who is responsible for stealing Claribel forevermore. Instead, I'm interested in the racist structures that perpetuate the idea that Blackness is foreign and foul. What is foul, from my perspective, is that Sebastian, along with Antonio, gives serious thought to murdering his own brother. He says:

> Thy case, dear friend,
> Shall be my precedent: as thou got'st Milan,
> I'll come by Naples. Draw thy sword. One stroke
> Shall free thee from the tribute which thou payest,
> And I the King shall love thee.

(2.1.332–6)

Where Antonio was willing to usurp and banish his brother Prospero, Sebastian is willing to kill his brother Alonso. These are the kind of men who see those darker of skin as less than human because they, themselves, lack humanity. Maybe there are no African-Caribbean freedom fighters in this play, but there sure are entitled, racist, inhumane white men, and that includes Prospero.

The reason much of this is important, from my perspective, is that the play offers us various aspects of social and racial inequities with an invitation to interrogate the structures that sustain them. If audiences, even for a moment, consider the Boatswain's candid take in the opening scene of the play they will readily recognize that the play scrutinizes hierarchies and renders them useless. The superiority of certain individuals over others is imagined, just as the god-like quality that Caliban sees in the drunken men is also imagined. What is not imagined in the play, in Shakespeare's world, nor in ours is the racism that is all too real.

I use *The Tempest* as a touchstone for this chapter's attention to solidarity between Black and brown not only because Caliban has so often been used as a stand-in for anyone other-than-white in the popular imagination, but also because he faces the harshest oppression in the play. In other words, across a broad multicultural/multiracial spectrum, writers, directors, actors, critics, and readers have identified with the struggle—physical, psychological, cultural, linguistic, ideological, religious, and political—that Caliban's existence in the play represents. While I can draw from a number of examples, I want to focus on Indira Karamcheti's thoughtful take on why being identified as a would-be Caliban is significant for scholars who, as she states, "are blessed with the 'surplus visibility' of race or ethnicity."[12] In other words, those of us dark of skin are not imagined as Prospero "in charge of the books of magic," but instead as "Calibans, rough beasts slouching (maybe even shuffling) along in the ivied Bethlehems of higher education."[13] The predominance of whiteness in academia, in no uncertain terms, allows Karamcheti to arrive at this view.

The not so secret issue at hand is the wholesale Eurocentric backbone of our education system. Anything outside of that framework is seen, at best, as ancillary and a curiosity. We are made to believe that Sebastian's view of "our" Europe means everyone ought to see that as sacrosanct. But it isn't. Such a perspective, just like Sebastian, is racist. This is precisely what Karamcheti addresses in her interrogation of the association of those dark of skin with Caliban. Karamcheti writes:

> We are sometimes seen, it seems to me, as traveling icons of culture, both traditional (as long as we're over there) and nontraditional (when we're right here), unbearably ancient in our folk wisdom and childlike in our infantile need for the sophistication of the West. We are flesh and blood information retrieval systems, native informants

who demonstrate and act out difference, often with an imperfectly concealed political agenda. We are the local and the regional opposed to the universality of the West, nature to its culture, instinct to its intellect, body to its brain. We are, in fact, encased in the personal and visible facts of our visible selves, walking exemplars of ethnicity and of race.[14]

Karamcheti's perspective speaks to a broad range of experiences of expendability for people of color as it is germane to the expansive nature behind the "brown" I mention in the introduction. And yet, her view comes specifically as a brown woman teaching at a predominantly white university. For this Chicano, Karamcheti's experience is all too familiar.

The sophistication of the West is not universal, but instead it is so often suffocating and leads us to feel like we are just vulnerable Black and brown bodies. And if you are white and feel that you do not see us darker of skin in that way, I am here to say that recognizing that is not enough. Karamcheti has been made to feel this way. I have been made to feel this way. And the weight of whiteness has made us feel this way. We are not your Caliban—your "thing of darkness" (5.1.130).

But if we dark of skin are all, at some point, cast as would-be Calibans, shouldn't we all, like Caliban, use the language of the oppressor to curse and push back? Shouldn't we resist that oppression? Unlike Caliban, we don't have to do this alone, and we don't have to rely on the likes of Trinculo and Stephano. To come together and move forward in solidarity to call out the various oppressive structures that we encounter, with confidence and with honesty, is a first step. Without community, we operate in isolation, and that is a burden much too heavy for any of us to bear.

I want to point, then, to both an early moment in the play to consider the heaviness of Caliban's existence. Early in the play, Caliban describes his history with Prospero as follows:

> This island's mine by Sycorax, my mother,
> Which thou tak'st from me. When thou cam'st first,
> Thou strok'st me and made much of me, wouldst give me
> Water with berries in 't, and teach me how
> To name the bigger light and how the less,
> That burn by day and night. And then I loved thee,
> And showed thee all the qualities o' th' isle,
> The fresh springs, brine pits, barren place and fertile.
> Curse be I that did so! All the charms
> Of Sycorax, toads, beetles, bats, light on you,
> For I am all the subjects that you have,
> Which first was mine own king; and here you sty me
> In this hard rock, whiles you do keep from me,
> The rest o' the' island.
>
> (1.2.395–411)

Caliban's memories are tender, and when he admits, "And then I loved thee," it should kill us all as readers. His description, of course, reflects how the Indigenous nations of the Americas were exploited by colonists. But the description also serves to infantilize those who are seen to be represented by Caliban. Resistance to the colonizing efforts of the Europeans was and is vividly real.

I want, once again, to cast the spotlight on the oppressor— to see the monstrosity of Prospero. Given the exchange of knowledge between Caliban and Prospero here, what strikes me as significant is that Caliban trades what was given to him by his mother (the island) to what was given to and taken away from him by his would-be father (false tenderness and love). To that end, when he says, "All the charms / Of Sycorax ... light on you," he confidently reclaims that which made and continues to make him. He draws on his mother's power, on his history, and that which predates the arrival of Prospero on that island. Still, it is the likes of Prospero and Miranda who keep him enslaved, who whip him, who torture him, and who keep him from that which belongs to him.

And isn't this the claim we have on our own country? Don't we, Black and brown, have as much right to the freedoms, justice, and peace of mind that we exist in a country that will not discriminate? We are always rendered suspect. To be Black and bird watching, reading in a shared public space, or simply doing yardwork in your own front yard can be precarious in our nation. To speak Arabic, Hindi, or Spanish is to draw the ire of so many in our plural society. To wear a hijab is seen as an affront to the perceived freedoms that so many hold so dear (that is, as long as they align with whiteness). And all of the above-mentioned situations can and do so often escalate into violent confrontations. There are so many would-be Prosperos who seek to suffocate us. We need to remember that our histories precede theirs. We need to invest in ourselves.

The real tragedy is that so many in our nation choose to abide by a selective consciousness when it comes to the realities of racism. This is why, I feel, a praxis of solidarity for Black and brown people is such a necessary starting point. Under that design, I wholeheartedly believe that those who are white and committed to antiracist efforts will follow our lead. For me, Anzaldúa comes to mind here, as she says of us Chicanxs, "how patient we seem, how very patient."[15] Patience, endurance, suffering, resilience, waiting—all of these, of course, are terms so often applied to the experiences of oppression for Black and brown people. But Anzaldúa, like Karamcheti, is thinking of her own experiences. She goes on to write of Chicanxs:

> We know how to survive. When other races have given up their tongue, we've kept ours. We know what it is to live under the hammer blow of the dominant *norteamericano* culture. But more than we count the blows, we count the days the weeks the years the centuries the eons until the white laws and commerce and customs will rot in the deserts they've created, lie bleached.[16]

It is a story of perseverance in the face of seemingly unending oppression, and it certainly stems beyond the experiences of Chicanxs. The hammer blow, the white laws, and the white customs have far-reaching effects. Indeed, later Anzaldúa says of the widespread struggle, "We need to meet on a broader communal ground."[17] Like Fluellen, like Caliban, we cannot go it alone.

When we recognize that the way the structures of power are currently set up, we see in them the lie that King Henry tells his men. We are asked to believe that we all belong to this nation, but so many of us are excluded at every turn. Our names don't matter to many, and indeed many can't bother to pronounce our names correctly. Here, in this moment, we can find no band of brothers in that fictitious sense of national belonging. But in resisting and pushing back on those oppressive structures, we might in fact find and forge a community worth investing in. Together, let's count the blows. Let's count the days. Let's count the weeks, and years, and centuries. Let's keep receipts. If our experiences of expendability are truly shared, let's share in efforts to make sure we are no longer expendable.

NOTES

1   Sir Philip Sidney, "The Defense of Poesy," *The Norton Anthology of English Literature,* Vol. B, 10th ed., ed. Stephen Greenblatt, et al. (New York: W.W. Norton), 581

2   Márquez, "Juan Crow: Progressive Mutations of the Black-White Binary," *Critical Ethnic Studies: A Reader,* ed. Nada Elia, et al. (Durham, NC: Duke UP, 2016), 48.

3   Ibid., 49.

4   Ibid., 48.

5   Ibid., 51.

6   Simone Wilson, "Angela Davis Says Black People Have a Responsibility to Support the Dream Act," *Migrare / Migrate / Change,* February 28, 2012. https://migrare.wordpress.com/2012/03/01/angela-davis-says-black-people-have-a-responsibility-to-support-the-dream-act

7   Derrick Bell, "Who's Afraid of Critical Race Theory?" *University of Illinois Law Review,* 1995: 898.

8   William Shakespeare, *The Tempest,* ed. Barbara A. Mowat and Paul Werstine (New York: Folger Shakespeare Library, 1994).

9   Harold Bloom, *Shakespeare: The Invention of the Human* (New York: Riverhead Books, 1998), 662.

10 Ibid., 662.

11 I am indebted to Bernadette Andrea, who, in her stunning talk, "'A Swarthy Group of Strangers': Shakespeare, Islamophobia, and Race," at the 2019 Meeting of the Shakespeare Association of America in Washington D.C., pointed out the seemingly obvious and yet often overlooked fact that Tunisia is much closer in proximity to Naples than Milan.

12 Indira Karamcheti, "Caliban in the Classroom," *The Radical Teacher* 44 (Winter 1993): 13.

13 Ibid., 13.

14 Ibid., 14.

15 Gloria Anzaldúa, *Borderlands/La Frontera: The New Mestiza* (San Francisco: Aunt Lute Books, 1987), 85.

16 Ibid., 85–6.

17 Ibid., 109.

Six

When the First Lord tells Duke Senior and other courtiers the story of Jacques' melancholic reaction to a murdered stag in *As You Like It*, the humorous tale takes a serious turn once the language of citizenship is employed. As a "careless herd, / Full of the pasture" passes the dying stag, Jacques is said to remark, "Sweep on, you fat and greasy citizens! / 'Tis just the fashion. Wherefore do you look / Upon that poor and broken bankrupt there?" (2.1.55–60). Because the story comes on the heels of Duke Senior suggesting that he and his men "go and kill us venison" (2.1.21), attention to Jacques' empathy for the dying animal provides a counterpoint that ought to ring comedic.

But the personification of the careless herd carries with it some biting commentary on the indifference that greedy citizens, both in the court and in the country, exhibit. As the Lord goes on to say of Jacques' criticism,

Thus most invectively he pierceth through
The body of country, city, court—
Yea, and of this our life, swearing that we
Are mere usurpers, tyrants, and what's worse,
To fright the animals and to kill them up
In their assigned and native dwelling place.

(2.1.61–6)

You must recall, Duke Senior is a man who sought refuge in the forest, who sees these men as "brothers in exiles," and who "Finds tongues in trees, books in the running brooks, / Sermons in stones, and good in everything" (2.1.1, 16–17). Their new pastoral environment, the liminal space that they inhabit, has something to teach them, but respect for this environment seems to have its limits. Much too often, it is easy to ignore the suffering of others, and these men are being asked to consider precisely that. More importantly, they are being asked to consider their own roles in the exploitations of those they are displacing.

We can recognize in the act of indifference to the suffering stag that Jacques condemns our own tendencies to dismiss such suffering when it comes to the long brutal history of colonialism and colonized peoples. In the settler colony that is the United States, the greed and tyranny that led to widespread genocide and slavery are defining facets of the fabric of this nation. The continued indifference to the suffering of Indigenous Peoples and Black Americans, too, is a defining facet of the fabric of this nation. The history of inhumanity and the inhumanity of our historical present are only possible because of such indifference. This chapter considers how, as a nation with a deep history of racism and abuses of human rights that has nonetheless fashioned itself as a land of exceptionalism, we often ignore in our historical present the violated Black and brown people residing not only in our country but also in regions beyond. Whether it be the femicides in Ciudad Juárez, Mexico, the killing of unarmed Palestinian protestors at the Gaza border, Haitian displacement, human rights violations in Darfur, or government-sanctioned murders in the Philippines, acts of terror and tyranny in the not so distant past are often met with apathy. Those human rights abuses feel far off, and yet we need to recognize that they are not unlike the ongoing human rights violations in our own nation. Of more importance, we need to be vividly aware that our own government has time and time again exhibited indifference to suffering when it comes to Black and brown people—both here and elsewhere. This chapter draws on Shakespeare not only to explore the relevance of the danger of that indifference in our current moment but also to put under the spotlight the repulsive political bodies that capitalize on the suffering of those who are Black and brown.

Since the 2016 U.S. presidential election, disdain for those Black and brown of skin has been a hallmark of the White House, and many within the United States proudly wear their racism on their sleeve. Why, Donald Trump is said to have asked at a White House meeting, should the United States accept immigrants from "shithole countries" when we could be bringing in people from places like Norway?[1] One day prior to making these statements where he identified those "shithole countries" as Haiti, El Salvador, and African countries, Trump met with the Prime Minister of Norway. His statement should give us pause because the level of obscenity and racism behind this is absolutely appalling, but it is something so many of us have come to expect from Trump. The belief that whiteness reigns supreme when it comes to the perceived value of U.S. citizens and notions of national belonging stems far beyond the White House.

Such overt white supremacist sentiments, then, ought to mobilize antiracist efforts across our nation and across color lines. However, even those sympathetic to issues of racial justice sometimes feel powerless when confronted with views like this and with the widespread human rights abuses against Black and brown individuals that transpire on a consistent basis. Often, indifference begins to settle in and thus we turn inward. Such insularity, of course, becomes incredibly dangerous because it sustains systems of oppression. Do we, like the well-fed, greasy citizens of Jacques' imagination simply sweep on? In my opening chapter, I mention how many of us likely saw images of the lifeless body of Michael Brown irreverently left on the hot asphalt in Ferguson, Missouri in full view, and yet many have since then failed to look back at that awful injustice. As we know, though, the murder of unarmed Black men and women is recursive. At no point in our nation's history do we need to look that far back to find examples of this awful, racist violence. That is our national tragedy. That is our nation's legacy. We might shake our head at it, voice support on social media, express our outrage to family and friends, but ultimately do we change our Black Lives Matter profile picture and then move on? This is our reality, because our justice system fails to hold murderers with police badges accountable. Collectively, we know this, but the majority of the populations does not want to buy into wholesale reform. The narrative of "a few bad apples" surfaces when it comes to cops, and even though many people know better, they buy that because the skin they're in doesn't put them in life or death situations when getting pulled over and hoping that the police officer is not one of the bad apples. And so, slowly that reluctance turns to indifference, and we sweep on. 'Tis just the fashion.

Of course, this indifference does not simply apply to the police killings I discuss in previous chapters. After Trump was elected, Saturday Night Live (SNL) capitalized on absurd aspects of his persona and administration and decided to bring Alec Baldwin's impersonation of Trump to the small screen. By making Trump a "running joke," many thought this move to bring Baldwin onto the show might prove "consequential."[2] Maybe. But for me, Baldwin's talented, satirical impersonation of Trump, although amusing, rings hollow because NBC and SNL helped propel the Trump machinery. Indeed, when Trump was running for president in 2015, SNL invited him to host their show. The Latinx community was in disbelief, and an array of Latinx groups including the Congressional Hispanic Caucus asked SNL to rescind their invitation because Trump had characterized Mexicans and Latinxs as "criminals and rapists."[3]

Lorne Michaels, SNL's Executive Producer, ignored these calls and hosted Trump on his show anyway. Without doubt, television ratings and not brown lives were on Michaels' mind. Latinx activists loudly protested Trump's appearance on the show outside of the NBC studio in New York, and it is said that you could hear the chanting from inside the studio. Amanda Terkel writes of the protest:

> Activists have been upset with NBC's decision to feature Trump not only for his divisive rhetoric about the Latino community, but also because "Saturday Night Live" has had very few Latino hosts and cast members over the years. In fact, just 19 of the 790 "Saturday Night Live" episodes over the past 40 years have had a Latino host, and only two Latinos have ever been part of the full-time cast of the show.[4]

As I mention above, whiteness reigns supreme. The attention here to the near invisibility of Latinxs on SNL speaks volumes, as viewers are not invited to consider Latinxs voices or perspectives. Latinxs are whitewashed, and we get a vastly different view of Latinx identities, which I discuss later in this chapter. But in this SNL controversy, Lorne Michaels clearly chose ratings over an ethical stance on having a racist celebrity host his show. It is shameful. These protesters knew that giving Trump that airtime during a presidential election could have awful consequences. It did. And after Trump won the presidency, SNL employed Alec Baldwin to address it. Ratings surged.

It gets worse. In a March 2017 parody sketch on SNL, Scarlett Johansen portrayed Ivanka Trump, daughter of Trump and a member of his administration, promoting a perfume called "Complicit." It sought to criticize the fact that Ivanka identifies herself as a feminist and yet so often defends and works to promote her father, whose misogyny is well known.[5] Audiences ate this up, as it cast light on the hypocrisy of Ivanka Trump. It was a clever and pointed move by SNL, but I readily recognized the irony of SNL calling someone out for being complicit. If the network sought to parody this in an effort to show the hypocrisy of those willing to overlook the ample deficits of Trump to promote themselves, then I could not think of anyone more fitting to pander this hollow message than Lorne Michaels. Perhaps Michaels should have stood alongside Ivanka to sell that perfume. The complicity of SNL and all who were willing to overlook the obscenity of Trump's racism for the sake of entertainment felt heavy. If we're being honest, Michaels was complicit in getting the racist Trump elected. How many people tuned in to watch Trump on SNL? How many felt it was not such a big deal? It was, and it continues to be a big deal. The truth is, it shouldn't have been just Latinxs protesting that show. Collectively, more people should have been disgusted by his racist rhetoric and refused to tune in to see him on a comedy show or anywhere else. Instead, many were indifferent to those protesting outside the NBC studios. I don't pretend that Trump is the root of racism in America, but I also will not overlook the large role he has in motivating violent acts of racism.

Trump is racist, SNL was complicit in that racism, and viewers okay with SNL's complicity in that racism sustained those structures of racism. Perhaps people simply want to tune in to entertaining programming, and I get it—I really do. I, too, sometimes tune in to watch mediocre television that delivers a few good laughs, but when it comes to giving a racist man who is running for the highest office in our nation airtime in a way that will present him as relatable, we can simply say "no." If we start to resist there, then there is the hope we can effect change on a larger scale. This is why I use Jacques' commentary in *As You Like It* above, because, in many ways, I think his thoughtful take in that play underscores how indifference and complacency allow the awful realities of racism to persist. This is to say, although Jacques is not addressing racism, he is looking at the world through eyes unwilling to pretend that social inequities are not a reality. Indeed, at the end of the play, Jacques is deliberate about leaving behind such a society and is intent on seeking out others who have rejected the "pompous court" (5.4.188).

The truth, of course, is that Jacques is not necessarily taken seriously by others in the play, and his decision to walk away from a social structure with which he disagrees is a very minor point in the comedic resolution to that play. He is on the outside looking in as others in the play happily anticipate returning to a court defined by hierarchies and uncompromising views that some people are born superior to others. As an audience, we ostensibly celebrate that, too. We might not take time to question how resolution in Shakespeare's comedies almost always equates to a return to predictable, and inequitable social structure—structures that favor the few. We need to scrutinize those structures in the play and the structures in our contemporary society and not simply accept them as a given.

However, the difficulty of imagining substantial change when it comes to social and racial inequities much too often seems far-fetched, and the feeling of disempowerment settles in like a toothache. I think, very deliberately, about the way the Trump administration has mobilized anti-immigrant attitudes and policies to inflict abuse not only against Latinxs seeking a better life in the United States but those who have spent their lives here and who call the United States their home. I think about the family separations at the U.S. Mexico border, the indefinite incarceration of immigrants and asylum seekers who are dark of skin, and the stories of abuse that have emerged from the awful shadows of those detention camps. I think of these things, and wonder what else, beyond the act voting, can be done? My congresswoman is on the same page as me, so calling her is preaching to the choir. My senators have ignored my kind their entire lives, even if one of them is a Latino, albeit one full of self-hatred. The uses of Shakespeare seem so trivial in those moments. It is one thing for people to come together and recite passages from Shakespeare in an act of solidarity with immigrants, as I discuss in Chapter 2, but it is something altogether different for me to sit in my house in *la frontera* knowing that a short drive away from my comfortable home brown children are wondering if they'll ever see their parents, their homeland, or the outside of that camp again. It is a toothache that keeps me awake and makes me want to dismantle, forcefully, every structure that has allowed them to be caged.

As I mention in the previous chapter, Gloria Anzaldúa says of Chicanxs in the face of their struggle against paradigms of white supremacy: "How patient we seem. How very patient."[6] The force of Anzaldúa's use of "seem" here rivals Hamlet. Without doubt, so many who see themselves as superior to us Chicanxs expect from us a particular passivity. But Anzaldúa goes on to say of Chicanxs:

> *Humildes* yet proud, *quietos* yet wild, *nosotros los mexicanos*-Chicanos will walk by the crumbling ashes as we go about our business. Stubborn, persevering, impenetrable as stone, yet possessing a malleability that renders us unbreakable, we, the *mestizas* and *mestizos* will remain.[7]

The energies behind Anzaldúa's sentiments remain profoundly important when we consider the continued struggle against systems of oppression rooted in white supremacy. In her work, as the previous chapter details, Anzaldúa recognizes the unsustainability of the legal, economic, and cultural structures that privilege whiteness above all else, and highlights Chicanx resilience. But it is presented as a balancing act—humble, yet proud; quiet, yet wild; impenetrable, yet malleable. It is clear that we must adapt and cross borders to endure. But there is a point where I simply want to say, and where I think Anzaldúa is encouraging us to say, "I know not 'seems.'"

If we look away from the horrors transpiring in the present moment, then we are no better than the well-fed herd, the greasy citizens, of Jacques' imagination. We need to consider the harsh truth behind that from which so many in our nation are willing to look away. The children, as young as seven and eight, in these detention facilities "in Clint, Texas were sleeping on concrete floors and being denied soap and toothpaste," and at least one visiting doctor described the detention centers as "torture facilities."[8] The cruel treatment against immigrants is widespread:

At a processing center in El Paso, Texas, 900 migrants were "being held at a facility designed for 125. In some cases, cells designed for 35 people were holding 155 people," *The New York Times* reported. One observer described the facility to *Texas Monthly* as a "human dog pound." The government's own investigators have found detainees in facilities run by Immigration and Customs Enforcement being fed expired food at detention facilities, "nooses in detainee cells," "inadequate medical care," and "unsafe and unhealthy conditions." An early-July inspector-general report found "dangerous overcrowding" in some Border Patrol facilities and included pictures of people crowded together like human cargo. More than 50,000 people are being held in facilities run by ICE, and something close to 20,000 in facilities run by Customs and Border Protection, and more than 11,000 children in the custody of the Department of Health and Human Services. (The government describes them as "unaccompanied," a label immigration advocates say is misleading because many were separated by the government from the relative who brought them).[9]

The author of the article is quick to point out that this should not be compared to concentration camps in Nazi Germany, as some have suggested, because the crimes committed are "not genocide."[10] And yet, it does present to us something very close to concentration camps and this is outright frightening.

There is no denying the deliberate cruelty that undergirds the ideas behind immigration detention centers under the

Trump administration. Stephen Miller, the weak-minded architect behind much of Trump's anti-immigrant policies, is often a focal point of the cruelty enacted at these centers. Make no mistake about it, I am of the mindset that this small, racist man should be tried for crimes against humanity. He is repulsive. However, I do not want to put sole blame on Miller because, clearly, many other people in the administration, including Trump himself, bought into his ideas. The effects, though, are unbelievably disturbing. As Adam Serwer writes,

> If these facilities even vaguely resemble concentration camps, then American society has failed in ways many Americans do not want to contemplate. That resemblance would cast the Republican Party and its president as the perpetrators of an act of historic villainy. The Democratic Party leadership does not want the responsibility of leveling this charge and is incapable of bearing it, and most Republicans seem convinced that the omelet is worth a few cracked shells.[11]

I'll take it a step further. Republicans are fully comfortable with an omelet that is grotesquely littered with cracked shells. Their indifference has allowed so much of this to happen. They, too, are to blame. Their dissatisfaction with the camps rings hollow because, at every single turn, they have supported the Trump administration. The facilities too, without doubt, resemble concentration camps. Our government forced sterilization procedures on multiple migrant women in these camps, and it lost the parents of 545 detained migrant children.[12] Again, as with the moment I mentioned above when Trump positioned the value of white people from

Norway as desirable against dark-skinned people, undesirable people originating from "shithole countries," I want to pause here to underscore the full implications behind these realities. Our government forced surgeries on migrant women to sterilize them. These women had no choice. Our government separated 545 children from their parents and then lost them. To imagine what such a loss means to a young child, to a parent, to anyone with any sense of compassion is to recognize the failure of our nation. But, like many everyday citizens in Hitler's Nazi Germany, so many are simply apathetic to these horrors. They might not be camps rooted in designs for genocide, but given the forced sterilization surgeries, we are not far off. Our government is flirting with genocide. It is nothing short of terrifying.

The indifference to these realities is also terrifying. More often than not, I feel paralyzed by it all, and it is because a sense of powerlessness has set in. What I do know is that resistance is critical, and to date, there have been various protests against the camps, with specific attention to the practice of family separations. Without doubt, there are a number of organizations working to try to help the incarcerated immigrants, including the American Civil Liberties Union (ACLU), but the widespread racial and social injustices in which this administration has engaged make it difficult because the battles are being fought on multiple fronts. Because of this, our energies need to be collective and they need to be sustained, and the BIPOC community in particular needs to come together. There needs to be a point where we all say, "enough."

When I think of active resistance in Shakespeare, I am often drawn to a minor plotline in *Measure for Measure*, a play that demands a good deal of resistance. *Measure for Measure* offers us a truly horrific brand of misogyny and misrule. However, Barnardine, from that very play, provides us with a glimpse into active resistance that often flies below the radar. Barnardine is in prison and awaiting to be executed, but he outright refuses to go along with a warrant ordering his execution. When presented with the news that he is to be executed, Barnardine explains that he has been drinking all night and is "not fitted for 't" (4.3.45–6).[13] On the surface, there is something comical about his refusal to go along with the execution because he is hungover. Indeed, his executioners joke that he will be able to sleep much thereafter. However, it is what Barnardine says to the Duke, disguised as a Friar come to comfort him in his last hour, that I find compelling. The Duke (as Friar) says, "Sir, induced by my charity, and hearing how hastily you are to depart, I am come to advise you, comfort you, and pray with you" (4.3.52–5). Barnardine responds, "Friar, not I. I have been drinking hard all night, and I will have more time to prepare me, or they shall beat out my brains with billets. I will not consent to die this day, that's certain" (4.3.56–9). Somehow, the image of his jailors beating out his brains with billets paints for us a vividly violent picture. Either you leave me alone, he seems to say, or you'll have to kill me in a horrifically violent manner here. But isn't the execution itself also horrifically violent? Even if the act of executing a prisoner is so often, then and now, veiled as a ceremonious act of justice, the endgame of that act is the killing of a human being. What, then, is meant to be upsetting to his immediate audience when he evokes the possibility that they will have to dash his brains out, like Lady Macbeth and her imagined baby. Is it the act of resistance that magnifies the violence against the prisoner?

When we disrupt the expected course of governmental policies that devalue certain lives, we stand to draw attention to the vivid violence that results from the enactment of such policies. Barnardine ultimately says to the Duke, "I swear I will not die today for any man's persuasion" (4.3.64). He is outright confident in his refusal. It is akin, perhaps, to the Boatswain refusing to entertain the interruptions of the nobility during the opening storm in *The Tempest* that I discussed in the previous chapter. If you recall, Gonzalo's sharp response is that the look of the Boatswain is all gallows, and thus he is imagined to be worthy of execution. What we know about *The Tempest* is that the nobility is less than honorable, and what we know about the government in *Measure for Measure* is that it is duplicitous, tyrannous, and outright disgusting. Why, then, would someone simply go along with the rituals of their own execution? If one fights back and makes the executioners show deadly force—show themselves barbaric—like Barnardine suggests, it forces the audience to see that it is murder and not ceremony.

To be clear, I am not suggesting here that the incarcerated immigrants should take a stand like Barnardine. That is not my point. However, I do want us to consider the seemingly pedestrian stance on resistance that his example offers. For those of us citizens of this nation, it begins with a simple, "no." It begins by saying, with confidence, "no, this should not be happening." It should compel us to reach out to our elected representatives to take action. It should compel us to boycott any companies doing business with these camps. The spotlight should be consistently focused on the horrific injustice that is transpiring in those detention centers and at the border.

The injustice is not only firmly situated with U.S. Immigration and Customs Enforcement (ICE) but also with the immigration courts that clearly see the immigrants—including children—as inconsequential. Mazin Sidahmed explains:

> The Sixth Amendment guarantees and individual's right to counsel in criminal proceedings, but the government argues that the right does not extend to immigration courts, which are deemed civil despite the severity of the consequences considered. In a 2014 CNN opinion article, a nationally prominent immigration judge, Dana Leigh Marks of San Francisco, said the drama of immigration cases "often involves life and death consequences," making them amount to death penalty cases heard in traffic court settings."[14]

Therein is an accurate assessment of the way the Trump administration and the government see Latinx immigrants. Someone akin to a traffic court judge decides the fate of so many individuals. Lest you forget, these immigrants are trying to escape brutal situations in their homeland in hopes of forging better lives. It is supposed to be the narrative that our country embraces. But it isn't.

The unwelcome sign went up long ago in the United States, and there only seems to be heartache for immigrants arriving on our proverbial shores. In these immigration courts, children as young as three years of age are being asked to represent themselves.[15] The idea for these immigration judges is clear—their voices and the circumstances that led them here do not matter, so we should deport every single one of them. If it is death they face on the other side of things, then so be it. However, we know that it does not have to be this way. The psychological, emotional, and physical pain that our government inflicts on these immigrants is unconscionable, and yet the camps, the torture, the façade of an impartial judge, and the grotesque architects of these policies persist. What are we doing about it?

After 2017, I was traveling quite a bit for conference presentations and guest lectures, and I began to notice more often than not groups of brown children escorted through our airport in El Paso, Texas. I did not want to admit to myself that they were likely victims of family separations being relocated. It was jarring at first, and the frequency of it is what was truly repulsive. At every turn, I wanted to ask those adults escorting them what they were doing? I wanted to tell them that all of this was wrong. I wanted to ask the children, usually dressed in white t-shirts, navy blue khaki pants, with knock-off Vans slip-ons, if they were okay. I feared, always, that I would make things worse for them. What power did I have? What force could I use? In my arsenal, I had only a knowledge of Shakespeare and a heavy heart. I convinced myself that I was powerless. I regret, much too often, not telling those agents in plain-clothes that they were disgusting—to look them in the eye so that they could see I understood fully their monstrosity.

I once saw Beto O'Rourke at the El Paso International Airport shortly after I saw a group of such kids, and I went up to him—he was running for Senate at the time—to tell him that Texas needed him and that I hoped he would unseat the bigot Ted Cruz. I felt awful for the kids I had just seen. I distinctly remember the kids holding transparent gallon-size storage bags filled with what looked like snacks and supplies. I wondered how long this would hold them over. I wondered where they were headed and what and who they were leaving behind—possibly forever. I thought about the mundane act of pulling out such a Ziplock bag from its box in my kitchen cabinet, filling it with some leftover food or other, and not worrying about wanting. What terror did those kids feel in that moment as they held that bag in their hands? In that moment, I sought someone who held the power to enact change in the policies that were hurting, so very badly, my own people, which is why I approached Beto to tell him this. I'm not even remotely close to a fanboy when it comes to politicians (talented poets and musicians are another story). I did not mean to posit Beto as a white savior, but that is precisely what I did. I thought he could remedy the situation if he won, which was misguided, I know, because the system is so much larger than any single person. But I wanted someone, I didn't care who, so very badly, to save those kids. Voicing my support to him didn't make me feel better, but I had hope things might change. Ultimately, Beto lost, and also 545 children lost their parents. Sexual, psychological, and physical abuse permeated those camps. I delivered my talks. I went about my ways. We have not closed the camps. We have not abolished ICE. I still long for the day we will.

When we are made to feel that we are kept situated in spaces of silence, inaction, and seeming patience, then we can recognize the dangers of indifference at work. In those various moments when I walked through the El Paso International Airport, I should have been able to look at any other person in that very airport to ask, "Are you seeing this? This is not right. We need to do something." But I know that not everyone shares my disbelief. I know that not everyone cared where those kids were going or what their situation was about. In fact, some likely agreed with the policies being enforced. Most looked at those kids, tried not to make eye contact, and then kept moving. Was I, then, part of that careless herd?

The real fear of complicity still haunts me, because along with so many people here and elsewhere, I know that what is transpiring in regard to immigration detention centers is outright horrific. There should be more forceful pushback. For many, though, the narratives about Latinxs are enough to give them doubt about our value. The media, in particular, is implicated in this design. For example, Leo Chavez writes:

> Both the Latino Threat Narrative and struggles over the meaning of citizenship pervade media-infused spectacles where immigration or immigrants are the topic. Broadly speaking, events or public performances that receive an inordinate volume of media attention and public opinion become media spectacles. It is difficult to escape media coverage and the incessant "talk" about immigration. Border surveillance, reproduction, fertility levels, fears of immigrant invasions and reconquests, amnesty programs, economic impacts, organ transplants, and the alleged inability to assimilate Latino immigrants and their offspring are all fodder for media attention.[16]

This is why normalizing someone who campaigned on the slogan, "Build the wall," and who characterized Mexicans as criminal invaders capable of raping someone, by inviting him on to a comedy sketch show attracting millions of viewers is dangerous. When bombarded by stories that cast Latinxs as a threat, then sentiments that seek to vilify and exclude Latinxs might become palatable for some. This is to say, not everyone agrees with Trump's characterization of Latinxs, but the media does much to present Latinxs as a viable threat to the cultural integrity of the United States—whatever that is (hint: it's whiteness).

I have already addressed how the forced sterilization of women in immigration detention centers brings us dangerously close to genocide, and so I hope it is clear that ignoring the complicity of media in narratives that drive hostile views of Latinxs is irresponsible. Moreover, consuming such media narratives only helps perpetuate the damage such narratives offer. For his part, Chavez debunks the Latino Threat Narrative, but outside of academic circles, not many are necessarily reading his book. The Latino Threat Narrative persists.

The truth is that the idea of assimilation plays such a prominent role in systems of belief that seek to measure and define Latinx success in our nation. The value of Latinxs is gauged by their ability to speak English properly, to adapt to customs deemed acceptable, and to adhere to cultural behaviors that the few see fit. To begin with the idea that "we" (always not so subtle code for white people) in the United States are what everyone else should aspire to approximate is already a faulty and, if we're honest, racist place to begin. Why is assimilation such an important goal for immigrants? Why are we not able to imagine a plural society with a multiplicity of cultural beliefs, practices, etc.? We bring so much more than flavorful food to the table. The truth is, so many in our nations simply do not want to see us.

As a Chicano who has a PhD in English Literature and specializes in Shakespeare, I can confidently say that most see me as successfully assimilated into the "dominant" culture. However, that is obviously an oversimplified understanding of me, and more than anything, that speaks volumes to the currency that Shakespeare carries. As I hope I have demonstrated up to this point in the book, I am not aspiring to approximate whiteness. I feel more committed to using the currency that Shakespeare carries to cast the spotlight on Black and brown lives so that people who are invested in the desire for us to approximate whiteness will recognize the dangers behind such attitudes. Of more importance, I want them to recognize the real danger of indifference. In turning away from the oppressive structures that devalue the lives of those dark of skin, the oppressive structures calcify. To carry on with life in this nation as if nothing is wrong is to disregard a black man saying "I can't breathe," to ignore the crying of a child in a cage who pleads incessantly for her father, and to ignore the policies that have allowed and will continue to allow for these atrocities to happen. It is a collective voice of resistance that this moment demands. No one wants to assimilate into a society that turns its back on innocent lives.

For his part, James Baldwin considers practices of assimilation and the force they carry when we consider what it means to be American. He writes:

> The making of an American begins at that point where he himself rejects all other ties, any other history, and himself adopts the vesture of his adopted land. This problem has been faced by all Americans throughout our history—in a way it is our history—and it baffles the immigrant and sets on edge the second generation until today. In the case of the Negro the past was taken from him whether he would or no; yet to forswear it was meaningless and availed him nothing, since his shameful history was carried, quite literally, on his brow. [17]

So much is lost, Baldwin suggests, in the process of becoming American. The expectation that the immigrant must detach from their culture and history is understood but is an incredibly heavy burden for the immigrant to carry. What is it they give up, and what is it that they gain by becoming American? Of more importance, Baldwin seems to suggest, those who are dark of skin can never really reject their history in the process of becoming American because their dark skin will forever give them away. It is those who fail to scrutinize attitudes that see whiteness and all it represents as the standard who help sustain structures of white supremacy and the horrors that they engender.

The problem with adopting the vesture of this adopted land is that this nation consistently signals to the world its inhospitality and racism. When U.S. citizens say in regard to the injustices that Black and brown people in the United States face, "we are better than that," what they don't understand is that we dark of skin have no reason to believe that. When, exactly, has this nation been better than that? When have Black and brown people not been at a disadvantage in this country? When has this country shown that it is willing to confront its awful history of slavery and offer reparations? When? We *should* be better than that. But police brutality is not new. Racist presidents are not new. White privilege is not new. And, unfortunately, indifference to all of this is not new.

If, in *As You Like It*, Jacques is lamenting the indifference to the murdered stag, we need to recognize, once again, that in that backdrop, the Duke and his men are preparing to hunt and kill venison. In other words, his commentary bears directly on the community he inhabits. He speaks up against the transgressions he witnesses. While we stand by, innocent people are being disparaged, caged, and killed by our government, and all of us should see that as heartbreaking. By magnifying the isolation of the dying stag and underscoring, quite pointedly, the indifference of the other "citizens" who fail to acknowledge that affliction, Jacques is asking his audience to care. He is asking his audience to recognize how entitled they are. He is asking them not to be selfish or greedy. He is looking directly at the dying stag and speaking up for the suffering he witnesses. We need to do the same, because in the process of such continuous acts of violence and killing, what we are witnessing is the slow dying of our democracy. Without doubt, it is the indifference of his "brothers in exile" that leads Jacques to detach himself, and many of us have undoubtedly felt that sense of hopelessness. But if we recognize the dangers of indifference, perhaps we can also recognize the potency behind paying attention, speaking up and out, and looking to forge a community committed to antiracist efforts.

NOTES

1 Josh Dawsey, "Trump Derides Protections for Immigrants from 'Shithole' Countries," The Washington Post, January 12, 2018. www.washingtonpost. com/politics/trump-attacks-protections-for-immigrants-from-shithole-countries-in-oval-office-meeting/2018/01/11/bfc0725c-f711-11e7-91af-31ac729add94_story.html

2 Chris Jones, "Alec Baldwin Gets Under Trump's Skin," The Atlantic, May 2017. www.theatlantic.com/magazine/archive/2017/05/alec-baldwin-gets-under-trumps-skin/521433/

3 Ashley Parker, "Latino Groups Call on 'S.N.L.' to Drop Donald Trump," New York Times, November 3, 2015. www.nytimes.com/2015/11/04/us/latino-groups-call-on-snl-to-drop-donald-trump.html

4 Amanda Terkel, "Latino Activists Protest Donald Trump's SNL Appearance Outside NBC," Huffington Post, November 7, 2015. www. huffpost.com/entry/donald-trump-nbc_n_563e9a49e4b0b24aee4a 9836

5 Laura Bradley, "Ivanka Trump Really, Really Didn't Like S.N.L.'s 'Complicit' Clip," Vanity Fair, August 16, 2018. www.vanityfair.com/hollywood/2018/08/ivanka-trump-snl-complicit-sketch-reaction-omarosa-unhinged-scarlett-johansson

6 Gloria Anzaldúa, Borderlands/La Frontera: The New Mestiza, 4th ed. (San Francisco: Aunt Lute Books, 1987): 85.

7 Ibid., 85–6.

8   Adam Serwer, "A Crime by Any Name," *The Atlantic*, July 3, 2019. www. theatlantic.com/ideas/archive/2019/07/border-facilities/593239/

9   Ibid.

10 Ibid.

11 Ibid.

12 See, Maya Manian, "Immigration Detention and Coerced Sterilization: History Tragically Repeats Itself," *ACLU*, September 29, 2020. https://www.aclu.org/news/immigrants-rights/immigration-detention-and-coerced-sterilization-history-tragically-repeats-itself/; and, Scott Simon, "Parents of 545 Children Separate at U.S.-Mexico Border Have Not Been Located," *NPR*, October 24, 2020. www.npr.org/2020/10/24/927384388/parents-of-545-children-separated-at-u-s-mexico-border-have-not-been-located

13 William Shakespeare, *Measure for Measure*, ed. Barbara A. Mowat and Paul Werstine (New York: Folger Shakespeare Library, 1997).

14 Mazin Sidahmed, "It's Like an Automatic Deportation if You Don't Have a Lawyer," *The New York Times*, August 13, 2019. www.nytimes.com/2019/08/13/opinion/facing-the-injustice-of-immigration-court.html

15 See, for example, Hector Villagra, "The Injustice of Deporting Children Without Representation," *Los Angeles Times*, March 17, 2016. www.latimes.com/opinion/op-ed/la-oe-villagra-migrant-children-immigration-court-20160317-story.html

16 Leo Chaves, *The Latino Threat: Constructing Immigrants, Citizens, and the Nation* (Stanford, CA: Stanford UP, 2008): 5.

17 James Baldwin, *Notes of a Native Son* (Boston: Beacon Press, 1955): 30.

Shakespeare on the Shades of Racism

Seven

The title of Allen Ginsberg's "Howl" evinces Lear's painful cry when he holds his dead daughter Cordelia in his arms, but, for me, it is the opening line of that poem that powerfully evokes the figure of Lear. "I saw the best minds of my generation destroyed by madness," Ginsberg writes, "starving hysterical naked" (1–2).[1] The moment that comes to mind, of course, is when Lear suffers madness out in the storm and, after seeing a naked Edgar disguised as Poor Tom in a hovel, fully undresses himself. But the "starving hysterical naked" body stems beyond Lear's physical body and encapsulates the body of his nation. Indeed, it is while he is out in that storm that Lear reflects on his failures:

> Poor naked wretches, wheresoe'er you are,
> That bide the pelting of this pitiless storm,
> How shall your houseless heads and unfed sides,
> Your looped and windowed raggedness defend you
> From seasons such as these? O, I have ta'en
> Too little care of this. Take physic, pomp.
> Expose thyself to feel what wretches feel,
> That thou may'st shake the superflux to them
> And show the heavens more just.
>
> (3.4.32–40)

It is, in many ways, a moment where Lear physically feels the discomfort of living in harsh elements, and that brings to mind for him his subjects who are forced to suffer the storm because they lack a home and sustenance. Lear recognizes that he has taken "[t]oo little care of this." By feeling what they feel, Lear imagines an ability to offer his subjects what is superfluous to him—that is, to share the comforts of his vast wealth.

The truth, of course, is that Lear no longer enjoys those comforts because he is no longer king at that point, and yet he acknowledges his failures when it comes to the inequities of his society. Those inequities—the luxury few are afforded at the expense of the many—call to mind the inequities in our society in the present moment. Like Shakespeare, Ginsberg's poem also stems far beyond the individual to recognize the suffering of many, and to articulate the collective "howl" of his society. We, too, in the present moment can perhaps recognize that the best Black and brown minds of our generation are being destroyed by madness. This is why I put Shakespeare's *King Lear* in conversation with Ginsberg's "Howl"—because in obviously distinct ways, both works address systems of oppression. Their cry, I believe, can be collective when considering the wretched of our day.

When we focus specifically on Lear's experience in the storm, though, we recognize therein fractured feelings of disenfranchisement, guilt, and an apprehension regarding the world he inhabits in that moment. It is in his empathetic moments when the burden of being is unveiled with its full weight. When Lear is encouraged to enter the hovel so as to escape the suffering in the storm, he asks at the threshold of that shanty: "Wilt break my heart?" (3.4.6). Heartbroken, Lear fears entering what is unknown. Symbolically, this registers apprehensions that so many feel about entering relationships, putting trust in others, believing in something, having hope, or entering the figurative unknown. One cannot help but wonder, "will it break my heart?" The short answer, of course, is "yes," as everything is temporary. And yet, despite knowing that one way or another we are bound to lose that which we love, when we actually experience that loss, we cannot help but howl. When we look beyond ourselves the way that Lear does, we recognize that for some citizens, the nation lets them down again and again. What is lost in the process of experiencing racism in its manifold manifestations is also heartbreaking. In this way, Lear's question rings loudly in our present moment. If you are Black or brown, make no mistake about it, your nation will break your heart.

So often, we turn to Shakespeare to see what his works stand to offer us in apprehending the pressing issues of our present moment. For some, this includes turning to Shakespeare as we seek a better understanding of race and racism. But that is never the approach that we, as scholars, should take, and as I hope this book has demonstrated, we can use Shakespeare as a vehicle but not as a source of some sense of universal truth. What we need is a better understanding of race and racism to understand Shakespeare and for him to remain relevant as we—scholars, educators, directors, actors, audiences, and readers—continue to shape his meaning anew. As I have argued elsewhere, we don't need him, but he certainly needs us.[2]

The many scholars producing timely and compelling work on Shakespeare and race are the future of our field, and it is heartening to see that the ShakeRace community—which includes the powerful work coming out of the Arizona Center for Medieval and Renaissance Studies RaceB4Race ongoing conference series[3]—consistently fosters an atmosphere of inclusivity and promotes antiracist pedagogies and research. Indeed, race studies of Shakespeare should be the entry point to studying Shakespeare in any given classroom.[4] By centering the topic of race in Shakespeare, we stand to engender important conversations about racism in our day—conversations that are absolutely necessary across the board. The promise behind this, as this concluding chapter argues, brings with it an unequivocal call for us in the field to acknowledge that critical race studies of Shakespeare must be the principal topic of our moment.

As I place the spotlight squarely on racism, it is also imperative to amplify the voices of Black and brown individuals because it shifts the way we think about Shakespeare's purchase in our day. In Chapter 2, I explored how the meaning of Edmund's contemplation of his illegitimacy took on greater significance if spoken by a Black actor, and indeed that should serve as an index of the value of adding voices of people of color to the Shakespeare machinery at large. I turn, then, to James Baldwin who underscores what he, as a Black writer, brings to the table when it comes to understandings of Shakespeare and Western art more broadly:

> I know, in any case, that the most crucial time in my own
> development came when I was forced to recognize that
> I was a kind of bastard of the West; when I followed the line
> of my past I did not find myself in Europe but in Africa. And
> this meant that in some subtle way, in a really profound
> way, I brought to Shakespeare, Bach, Rembrandt, to the
> stones of Paris, to the cathedral at Chartres, and to the
> Empire State Building, a special attitude. These were not
> really my creations, they did not contain my history; I might

search in them in vain forever for any reflection of myself.
I was an interloper; this was not my heritage. At the same
time, I had no other heritage which I could possibly hope to
use—I had certainly been unfitted for the jungle or the tribe.
I would have to appropriate these white centuries, I would
have to make them mine—I would have to accept my special
attitude, my special place in this scheme—otherwise I would
have no place in *any* scheme.[5]

The difficulty behind this divide, for Baldwin, meant a
sense of anger aimed not only at white people but also at
Black people for not producing, to his mind, the likes of
Rembrandt. "In effect," he writes, "I hated and feared the
world. And this meant, not only that I thus gave the world an
altogether murderous power over me, but also that in such
a self-destroying limbo I could never hope to write."[6] If you
think that Shakespeare, anyone, or anything else on that list
somehow saved Baldwin, you would be terribly mistaken.
Baldwin came to understand himself and his voice, and his
voice and talent rivals any on that list.

Engaging Shakespeare a bit more explicitly in his essay,
"Why I Stopped Hating Shakespeare," Baldwin addresses
both the reasons for disconnecting from Shakespeare and his
ability later in life to find value therein. Although Baldwin
admits that his disdain for Shakespeare was in part because of
the "envy" he felt in regard to his "monstrous achievement,"
he goes on to say:

In my most anti-English days I condemned him as a
chauvinist ("this England" indeed!) and because I felt it so
bitterly anomalous that a black man should be forced to
deal with the English language at all—should be forced to

assault the English language in order to be able to speak—I condemned him as one of the authors and architects of my oppression.[7]

Baldwin recognizes the perceived authority of the English language, and this calls to mind the idea of language as a tool of oppression that both Pierre Bourdieu and Gloria Anzaldúa detail.[8] Because Shakespeare enjoys such an iconic status in the realm of English literature and indeed the popular imagination, it is understandable that his alignment with shaping the English language leads Baldwin to identify him as the architect of his oppression.

Despite his disdain for Shakespeare and English, though, Baldwin ultimately uncovers a reason to value both. However, his recognition of their merit is not a result of opening himself to allow the English language to shape him, but rather recognizing he might have something to bring to that language. Baldwin writes:

My quarrel with the English language has been that the language reflected none of my experience. But now I began to see the matter in quite another way. If the language was not my own, it might be the fault of the language; but it might also be my fault. Perhaps the language was not my own because I had never attempted to use it, had only learned to imitate it. If this were so, then it might be made to bear the burden of my experience if I could find the stamina to challenge it, and me, to such a test.[9]

To get there, Baldwin draws on his history with language that came from his "black ancestors, who evolved the sorrow song, the blues, and jazz" to create "an entirely new idiom in an overwhelmingly hostile place." Baldwin writes, "The authority of this language was in its candor, its irony, its density, and its beat: this was the authority of the language which produced me, and it was also the authority of Shakespeare."[10]

Baldwin's ability to connect his experience with jazz to his experiences with Shakespeare's language (and specifically its bawdiness) is accomplished only because he recognizes it in relation to himself and his history. This, he feels, is something Shakespeare's art stands to offer. Baldwin writes:

> The greatest poet in the English language found his poetry where poetry is found: in the lives of the people. He could have done this only through love—by knowing, which is not the same thing as understanding, that whatever was happening to anyone was happening to him. It is said that his time was easier than ours, but I doubt it—no time can be easy if one is living through it. I think it is simply that he walked his streets and saw them, and tried not to lie about what he saw: his public streets and his private streets, which are always so mysteriously and inexorably connected; but he trusted that connection. And, though I, and many of us, have bitterly bewailed (and will again) the lot of an American writer—to be part of a people who have ears to hear and hear not, who have eyes to see and see not—I am sure that Shakespeare did the same. Only, he saw, as I think we must, that the people who produce the poet are not responsible to him: he is responsible to them.[11]

What I find most compelling about Baldwin's exploration of his relationship with Shakespeare is that he does not adopt a view of Shakespeare's universality, but instead he recognizes that, through an understanding of himself and his own experience, Shakespeare can begin to speak a language that speaks meaningfully to him. It begins with the self.

It is not of minor significance, either, that Baldwin employs the word "love" to imagine Shakespeare's ability to see, to hear, and to know the importance of the lives of the people who surrounded him. In our moment, such love, if you want to call it that, or empathy is incredibly powerful in trying to forge an ethics of hospitality. We cannot just resign ourselves to the idea that the effects of racism are inevitable. Racism will persist, and I am not so naïve as to believe otherwise; but we need to move the marker beyond a celebration of resilience in the face of that racism. Baldwin, for example, considers the fraught nature of the way one reacts to social and racial inequities:

> It began to seem that one would have to hold in the mind forever two ideas which seemed to be in opposition. The first idea was acceptance, the acceptance, totally without rancor, of life as it is, and men as they are: in the light of this idea, it goes without saying that injustice is a commonplace. But this did not mean that one could be complacent, for the second idea was of equal power: that one must never, in one's own life, accept these injustices as commonplace but must fight them with all one's strength.[12]

The need to push back is obvious, and for those of us who teach Shakespeare, we can produce a poet whose work lends itself to antiracist efforts. By this, I don't mean that we need to fashion Shakespeare as progressive, but we can draw on the experience that we know—the place where our public streets and our private streets intersect—and shape a Shakespeare who allows us, with our voices, to bring awareness to the shades of racism in our day.

When Kim F. Hall and Peter Erickson put together the only special issue on race and Shakespeare in our field's top journal, *Shakespeare Quarterly*, in 2016, they were keenly aware of the fact that many, if not most, readers of that journal would be uneasy not only with the topic of race but also with the voices of scholars of color. But Erickson and Hall were clear about the value of these voices:

> What you are hearing in this issue is a desire to sing a new scholarly song, to embrace our strange style and our unseemliness in the service of understanding how early moderns as well as contemporary peoples "apprehend and engage in the historical relations of power and violence that permeate their particular everyday." In pursuing Thompson's astute activation of "passing strange" and the term's multivalent meanings in the early modern English and contemporary American lexicon, we can refuse a scholarship that passes, that continues to identify with the confining assumptions of early modern scholarship, and that speaks only the language of our dominant culture. Instead, we can move to a new phase where we set our own questions and chosen methods that embrace strangeness, that refuse an artificial border between past and present, and that listen to the voices of the people of color.[13]

Without doubt, Erickson and Hall have, over the years, shaped a version of Shakespeare that so many of us invested in critical race studies have found worth engaging. At its heart, here, Erickson and Hall make clear that deviating from understandings of Shakespeare that are self-perpetuating and always anchored in the language of the dominant culture stands to open up and revitalize Shakespeare and early modern studies with voices that have been largely unfamiliar. As we look forward, I firmly believe that it will be evident to most that these are the voices, these are the people who produce the poet that is worth our time.

Like Baldwin, Erickson and Hall highlight the fact that the personal experiences are what matter most in engaging the works of Shakespeare. At the 2019 Meeting of the Shakespeare Association of America (SAA) in Washington, D.C., Kim F. Hall delivered a talk on the Plenary Panel, "Looking Forward: New Directions in Early Modern Race Studies," that was nothing short of breathtaking.[14] She described her talk as "a personal meditation" focused on locating references to Othello in archives "meant to celebrate white achievement."[15] What the audience came to discover is that this meditation focused mostly on her work in the archives at the Schomburg Center for Research in Black Culture on the day after Donald J. Trump was elected to the office of president in 2016. In those archives, Hall was looking over a book of inventory that once belonged to New York Governor John Montgomerie, and interspersed within various objects that Montgomerie owned, Hall finds the names of young slaves—his inventory. Two pages in, Hall finds listed in the inventory a reference to a young boy named Barbados, who, together with Othello and two pipes of old Madeira wine, make up the most expensive items on the list; and yet, as Hall says, "they are worth a lot, but are they worth anything?"[16] This is the beautiful and painful poignancy of Hall's work. As the talk moves forward, her clear investment in the lives of these Black men—or more accurately, these Black boys—overshadows the fact that the archives preserved there seem to preserve the memory of these white slave owners. All of this transpires on the day after a large portion of our nation (and yet not the majority) voted into office a racist, misogynistic, hateful man who evokes for many, including me, the plantation owners that Hall is confronting. Yet she is there, emotionally invested, heartbroken, looking for Othello—finding young Black lives worth finding.

Most of us likely cannot begin to understand what the weight of such research in the archives must feel like when you're looking for a connection to Shakespeare but really looking at the way the white world has dehumanized your own, both then and now, and directly after a known racist was elected to the highest office in our nation. Hall captures that masterfully. As I listened to Hall's talk at the SAA, sitting in the second row of a full conference room with upwards of one thousand people in the audience, I found it difficult to hold back tears. Listening to the intermittent sniffling in that room, I knew I was not alone.

It feels easy in moments like that to think that people—people who share your intellectual interests, who engage in similar professional activities, and who you consider your scholarly community—actually care. Listening to her talk, how could they not? Hall says:

> I had originally intended this project as a way to explore what
> Francesca Royster called "Shakespeare with a difference"—
> to offer to the Shakespeare world another lens for thinking
> about Shakespeare in the 21st century. Item: one large
> decanter. But this feels like a foolish endeavor when it is
> clear for the foreseeable future our need is to build and
> support Black institutions and Black people. But I feel like
> I have to keep reading, to strain my eyes and agitate the

> arthritis in my back, because I need to find all of the Black
> people and sit still with the actual lives scattered amidst the
> stuff of Montgomerie's life. Item: lye tubs. To honor them
> and the survival of Black people needed but not wanted on a
> week when a huge portion of our country made it clear that
> we people of color are here only as we are needed.[17]

We should not forget that, for many scholars of color working on early modern race studies, the long legacy of racism is intricately connected to their everyday lived experiences. We don't have the luxury of peering in and then tuning out. And Hall's voice—her articulation of what it was like to work in the archives on lives that matter while a man who actively discriminates against Black and brown people and has made it known that he sees them as less valuable—makes all the difference in bringing meaning to Shakespeare. Her approach underscores an ethics of care, and it makes you wonder how many others working in the archives seek to see those lives. If so, what do they see. If not, why not?

When Kent receives word that Cordelia received his letter outlining the plight of Lear since her departure to France, he eagerly awaits to hear how she reacted. He wants to know if the suffering of her father moved her, and he wants to see if her empathetic potential remains in place after she had been publicly wronged by her father. He asks the Gentleman in attendance, "Did your letters pierce the Queen to any demonstration of grief?" (4.3.10). The Gentleman responds:

> Ay, sir, she took them, read them in my presence.
> And now and then an ample tear trilled down
> Her delicate cheek. It seemed she was a queen

Over her passion, who, most rebel-like,
Fought to be king o'er her.
                    (4.3.12–16)

Kent then says, "O, then it moved her," to which the Gentleman responds: "Not to a rage. Patience and sorrow strove / Who should express her goodliest" (4.3.19–20). In a world where tyranny and betrayal seem to define the experiences of many, Kent seeks to know that compassionate individuals remain. He desires to hear how Cordelia reacted. He wants to know that she was moved by the news. The Gentlemen, though, wants to underscore that her reaction falls within expected norms of sorrow. She does not overreact, but she is not cold in her reaction. Much of this, of course, is anchored in early modern Protestant expectations of the way one should grieve.[18] But for any audience across temporal borders, this also draws attention to the fact that there is no right way to grieve. Rage would have been understandable. Indeed, Lear's "howl" near the end of the play is understandable. And so, Kim F. Hall admitting that she struggled to hold back tears in those archives, and her audience at the SAA holding back tears in that conference room, show that the widespread vicious effects of racism deserves our grief. Everyone should be moved by it. Everyone should be motivated to act on it. Everyone.

However, apathy, as I argued in the previous chapter, often defines the reactions by the larger community. But the Black Lives Matter movement has done much to keep attention sustained on the racism that permeates our society, and it compels so many to look and look again. Despite the All Lives Matter and Blue Lives Matter attempts to diminish the force of what Black Lives Matter demands—that is, for our society to recognize that in our world, the lives of Black people matter less in the minds and actions of many, and as such puts them in a precarious state of existence—the movement persists. The truth is that the recursive acts of violence against unarmed Black men and women at the hands of police officers demand the continued efforts of the Black Lives Matter movement.

In the aftermath of the killing of Michael Brown, Black Lives Matter protests erupted because, once again, many Americans felt that enough was enough. But if one is Black in America, it has always felt this way. Nothing seems to give. Still, the fight persisted, and in the large community of protesters—not just Black protesters—there was a sense that this movement would not diminish. Amid those protests, as Fernando Orejuela tells us, "The hook from Kendrick Lamar's 2015 song, 'Alright,' was incorporated into a chant that reverberated at marches and demonstrations nationwide and was adopted as one of the most prevalent anthems of the Black Lives matter movement."[19] In that hook, Lamar sings, "We gon'be alright! We gon' be alright!"[20] It offers hope within a song that engages the constant struggle for Black people in the United States. Indeed, Lamar looks head on at the systemic violence against Blacks:

Wouldn't you know
We been hurt, been down before, n----
When our pride was low
Lookin' at the world like, "Where do we go, n----?"
And we hate po-po
Wanna kill us dead in the street for sure, n----
I'm at the preacher's door

My knees getting' weak and my gun might blow
But we gon' be alright.[21]

The term "po-po" refers to the police, and as such the "hurt" and the lack of "pride" of which he sings is directly correlated to the violence at the hands of police. The absence of belonging and the feeling that this nation is not one's home lead to the knock at the preacher's door because, holding a gun, the speaker wants to harm someone or harm himself. Given that intimation of suicidal thoughts later in the song, the latter is most likely. As listeners, we should feel the gravity behind that.

In the aftermath of the murder of Michael Brown, then, many found in Lamar's song the pain they were feeling, but also the necessity to exclaim with confidence that they would be alright. It is like Lear looking into the dark opening of the hovel and asking if it will hurt him—looking into the world that still holds him, maybe, and wondering if it will hurt him. And as I said before, the answer is, "yes." In a similar vein, racism and violence awaits many who are dark of skin in this nation built on slavery and genocide. The reach of anti-Blackness is immeasurable, and as such it is difficult to simply say that everything is going to be alright, which is not what Lamar does. He keeps things honest, but he also recognizes the need for confidence in the face of that oppression.

That sense of confidence, of course, is necessary in resisting the oppressive structures of white supremacy but so often difficult to instill in younger people of color because the world consistently demonstrates an irrational hatred toward them. As Ta-Nehisi Coates notes, "racism is a visceral experience," one that "dislodges brains, blocks airways, rips muscle, extracts organs, cracks bones, breaks teeth."[22] Young people see this. Coates' son saw this.

Reflecting on a television interview where he was asked what it meant to lose his body, Coates describes the sadness he felt at the end of the interview because he saw in it an absence of hope. That feeling lingers. He then addresses his 15-year-old son:

> That was the week you learned that the killers of Michael Brown would go free. The men who had left his body in the street like some awesome declaration of their inviolable power would never be punished. But you were young and still believed. You stayed up till 11 P.M. that night, waiting for the announcement of an indictment, and when instead it was announced that there was none you said, "I've got to go," and you went into your room, and I heard you crying. I came in five minutes after, and I didn't hug you, and I didn't comfort you, because I thought it would be wrong to comfort you. I did not tell you that it would be okay, because I have never believed it would be okay. What I told you is what your grandparents tried to tell me: that this is your country, that this is your world, that this is your body, and you must find some way to live within the all of it.[23]

Not having to negotiate the world like this—as a father, as a son, as Black man or woman—is what the term "white privilege" means. As a reader, as a Chicano, as a man whose skin is dark and who has felt a fair share of hostility and recognized in the looks and words of many a clear perception that I am inferior, I cannot even begin to understand the weight of what Coates describes. Anti-Blackness abounds, and thus the struggle "to live within the all of it" is both private and public. If we want to commit to antiracists efforts, if we want to build a coalition—the kind of praxis of solidarity that I mention in the previous chapter—it must begin with addressing anti-Blackness. It must begin there. If we recognize that Black lives matter, then we can move toward dismantling systems of white supremacy. Only then will it really be alright.

And yet, like many writers and thinkers who come at this, those possibilities seem remote to me. It isn't that I lack hope, but instead it is that I see in the words and actions of many of the citizens of this nation a grotesque comfort with the racism that surrounds us. If you have lingered in this chapter on the words of Baldwin, on the words of Hall, on the words of Lamar, and on the words of Coates, I wonder, then, if you will be able to close this book and tuck those words away on some shelf. Or will you let those words linger in you, feel their heavy beauty, and commit to antiracism in your daily lives?

So much and so many have been destroyed as a result of the widespread efforts to buttress a society that sustains white supremacy. From my corner of the world here on the U.S. Mexico border in El Paso, Texas, I see it in the faces and actions of our local government and business leaders, and I see it in the way the U.S. government inhumanely treats undocumented immigrants. In a city with over an 80% Chicanx population, predominantly white leadership remains, and social inequities that keep Chicanxs disempowered persist.[24] The weight of that, as I mentioned in my previous chapter, also feels unbearable at times. I know how my parents arrived here, and knowing that so many of the citizens of this country find no courage, no strength, no value in the stories or the lives of my parents and those like them often makes me wonder how much these same individuals must possess a self-hatred that they project so viciously to the world. For my part, I am trying to adopt a steady view of the many shades of racism we encounter without allowing it to harden my heart. As Baldwin writes about the struggle, "This fight begins ... in the heart and it now had been laid to my charge to keep my own heart free of hatred and despair."[25] Again, I am trying.

When Lear enters the final scene holding the dead body of Cordelia in his arms, he does not attempt to mask his heartache. "Howl, howl, howl," Lear wails, "O, you are men of stones!" (5.3.308). We can say the same about those who witness the vast injustices against those Black and brown of skin—who see on their television screens the dead bodies of men and women killed by police, brown children crying in cages, brown people kept in makeshift camps—and who simply do not care. When Lear feels the suffering of those who have no home, his subjects whom he recognizes he has disregarded, he begins to feel for them. And in this final scene, beginning with his entrance onstage, Lear focuses on his daughter—his dying words are infused with hope that she might still be alive. If we imagine ourselves as the keepers of our brothers and sisters, our grief should be no less. Our efforts to keep them alive should be no less.

As *King Lear* draws to a conclusion, Lear's immediate audience is left trying to make sense of the senseless violence and heartache that remains. Ultimately Edgar says:

> The weight of this sad time we must obey,
> Speak what we feel, not what we ought to say.
> The oldest hath borne most; we that are young
> Shall never see so much nor live so long.
>
> (5.3.392–5)

There is a poignancy behind each line that Edgar utters here. He encourages the audience to feel the weight of sadness—to feel the grief. Perhaps of most importance is his second line where he makes clear that we should speak from the heart, without fear of speaking our truth. This is something critical when we confront racial injustices in our time. The penultimate and final lines honor those who have come before and endured so much, and yet offer a muted hope for those who are young—for those who have not yet felt or endured so much. And yet those on the stage, including Edgar, did indeed see so much of that violence and heartache. Without doubt, those experiences might be markedly different across generations, but the cruelty and greed that undergird the world of King Lear remain to our present.

In the afterword to Luis Alberto Urrea's The Devil's Highway, which I discussed in Chapter 2, Urrea revisits the story of two of the victims—a father and teenage son—who were part of the tragic journey of the Yuma 14. "Of all the sad tales chronicled in my book," Urrea writes, "one has inspired the most sorrow and conversation. Reymundo Barrera Maruri. He and his son Reymundo Jr."[26] Describing the story of Reymundo Sr. as "so terrible" that he must approach it "in a state of prayer," Urrea explains that he was contacted by one of Maruri's family members after the publication of his book. Urrea writes:

> I was mortified when his nephew wrote to me. Not because he corrected something I had collected from the media— that he was indigenous. "Maruri is a mestizo name," the nephew wrote. No, I was deeply upset when he told me that none of his family knew the details of their fate until they found my book. He thanked me for writing the hideous story

of what happened to them, in all its agonizing detail. I was
mortified that I was the vector of such sorrow for a family
that had already been wounded. But he assured me that it
was healing to finally know the truth, after so much lying
from those involved.[27]

One can easily recognize the guilt that Urrea feels, but ultimately it is critical that he was able to tell a story that would
have otherwise been left untold and unknown to the victims'
family. And yet, for me, I cannot help but wonder how many
of these stories of the tragic loss of immigrants trying to find
their way to this inhospitable nation are lost. How many
stories of abuse ongoing at the detention centers will remain
untold and unknown? How many parents of the migrant children kept in camps have disappeared? How many children
have we lost?

I understand, then, the gratitude that Reymundo Barrera
Maruri's nephew felt. And this brings me to the end of Urrea's
story. He says of Maruri's nephew:

I will allow this good man to remain anonymous for now. But
I thought you'd like to know that earlier, he made the same
journey. For similar reasons. But he made it. Same paths.
   And he got an education. He got a Ph.D., in fact. And then
he went abroad as a scholar.
   He's a professor now. And a scholar in the area of world
economics. His plan: to find the way to save the border and
to heal relations between our nations.
   He wrote this to me: "I want the world to know what one
'wetback' can accomplish if given the chance."[28]

When I first read this afterword, this final anecdote brought
me to tears. I thought about my father's arduous journey to *la*

frontera as a young boy. The journey to this nation is way more precarious than it needs to be for many of those immigrants who are brown of skin—for those who do not originate from countries deemed desirable by a racist administration. The majority of these men and women simply want to find a better life, to build something for themselves, and to contribute meaningfully to the world in which they live. Indeed, a chance is precisely what is needed. But so many in this nation want only to foreclose on that promise because they see our presence here, they find in our brown faces, something that threatens what they feel belongs only to them. How do you heal something that has no heart?

In the face of all of this, I will readily admit that Shakespeare feels distant. I know that this book is supposed to put the spotlight on Shakespeare. But the spotlight needs to be put on the shades of racism that shape and define all of our lives. Like Kim F. Hall, I so often feel that I'm not here for Shakespeare. I want to sit with the injustice that surrounds me and my people and try to find a voice to howl.

NOTES

1 Allen Ginsberg, "Howl," *Howl and Other Poems* (San Francisco: City Lights Publishers, 1959).

2 See Ruben Espinosa, "Shakespeare and Your Mountainish Inhumanity," *The Sundial (ACMRS)*, August 16, 2019. https://medium.com/the-sundial-acmrs/shakespeare-and-your-mountainish-inhumanity-d255474027de

3 Anyone interested in conversations and resources surrounding critical race studies of Shakespeare should access the #ShakeRace hashtag on Twitter (you can access these conversations even if you are not on Twitter). For more information on RaceB4Race, see: https://acmrs.asu.edu/RaceB4Race

4 There are a number of works that underscore the value of race studies of Shakespeare and early modern literature, and although this list is by no means comprehensive, it does offer interested readers a starting point.

For the sake of manageability, I highlight one work by each author, but I strongly encourage readers to explore the wide array of compelling work these critics have produced. See, Patricia Akhimie, *Shakespeare and the Cultivation of Difference: Race and Conduct in the Early Modern World* (New York: Routledge, 2018); Dennis Britton, *Becoming Christian: Race, Reformation, and Early Modern English Romance* (New York: Fordham UP, 2014); David Sterling Brown, "Remixing the Family: Blackness and Domesticity in Shakespeare's *Titus Andronicus*," *Titus Andronicus: The State of Play*, ed. Farah Karim-Cooper (London: Arden Shakespeare, 2019): 111–33; Jonathan Burton, *Traffic and Turning: Islam and English Drama, 1579–1624* (Newark, DE: U of Delaware P, 2005); Urvashi Chakravarty, "More than Kin, Less Than Kind: Similitude, Strangeness, and Early Modern English Homonationalisms," *Shakespeare Quarterly* 67.1, 14–29; Vanessa Corredera, "'How Dey Goin' to Kill Othello?!': *Key & Peele* and Shakespearean Universality," *Journal of American Studies* 54.1, 27–35; Eric De Barros, "'Shakespeare on His Lips': Dreaming of the Shakespeare Center for Radical Thought and Transformative Action," *Teaching Social Justice Through Shakespeare*, ed. Hillary Eklund and Wendy Beth Hyman (Edinburgh, Scotland: Edinburgh UP, 2019): 206–14; Ambereen Dadabhoy, "Two Faced: The Problem of Othello's Visage," *Othello: The State of Play*, ed. Lena Cowen Orlin (London: Arden Shakespeare, 2014): 121–47; Peter Erickson, *Citing Shakespeare: The Reinterpretation of Race in Contemporary Literature and Art* (New York: Palgrave, 2007); Katherine Gillen, "Fashioning English Whiteness in *The Revenger's Tragedy*, *The Revenger's Tragedy: The State of Play*, ed. Linda Woodbridge (London: Arden Shakespeare, 2018): 113–33; Kyle Grady, "Othello, Colin Powell, and Post-Racial Anachronisms," *Shakespeare Quarterly* 67.1, 68–83; Kim F. Hall, *Things of Darkness: Economies of Race and Gender in Early Modern England* (Ithaca NY: Cornell UP, 1995); Margo Hendricks, "Gestures of Performance: Rethinking Race in Contemporary Shakespeare," *Colorblind Shakespeare: New Perspectives on Race and Performance*, ed. Ayanna Thompson (New York: Routledge, 2006): 187–203; Farah Karim-Cooper, *Titus Andronicus: The State of Play* (London: Arden Shakespeare, 2019); Arthur Little, *Shakespeare Jungle Fever: National-Imperial Re-Visions of Race, Rape, and Sacrifice* (Stanford, CA: Stanford UP, 2000); Joyce Green MacDonald, *Shakespearean Adaptation, Race and Memory in the New World* (New York: Palgrave, 2020); Carol

Mejia La Perle, "An Unlawful Race: Shakespeare's Cleopatra and the Crimes of Early Modern Gypsies," *Shakespeare* 13.3, 226–238; Noemie Ndiaye, "Aaron's Roots: Spaniards, Englishmen, and Blackamoors in *Titus Andronicus*," *Early Theatre* 19.2, 59–80; Francesca Royster, *Becoming Cleopatra: The Shifting Image of an Icon* (New York: Palgrave, 2003); Kathryn Vomero Santos, "Hosting Language: Immigration and Translation in *The Merry Wives of Windsor*," *Shakespeare and Immigration*, ed. Ruben Espinosa and David Ruiter (Burlington, VT: Ashgate, 2014): 59–72; Justin Shaw, "'Rub Him About the Temples': Othello, Disability, and the Failures of Care," *Early Theatre* 22.2, 171–83; Ian Smith, "Othello's Black Handkerchief," *Shakespeare Quarterly* 67.1, 95–120; Ayanna Thompson, *Passing Strange: Shakespeare, Race, and Contemporary America* (Oxford: Oxford UP, 2011); Sandra Young, *Shakespeare in the Global South: Stories of Oceans Crossed in Contemporary Adaptation* (London: Arden Shakespeare, 2019).

5 James Baldwin, *Notes of a Native Son* (Boston: Beacon Press, 1955): 6–7.

6 Ibid., 7.

7 James Baldwin, "Why I Stopped Hating Shakespeare," *The Cross of Redemption: Uncollected Writings* (New York: Vintage, 2011): 65.

8 See Pierre Bourdieu, *Language and Symbolic Power* (Cambridge, MA: Harvard UP, 1982), and Gloria Anzaldúa, *Borderlands/La Frontera: The New Mestiza* (San Francisco: Aunt Lute Books, 1999).

9 Baldwin, *The Cross of Redemption*, 67.

10 Ibid., 67–8.

11 Ibid., 68–9.

12 Baldwin, *Notes of a Native Son*, 114–15.

13 Peter Erickson and Kim F. Hall, "'A New Scholarly Song': Rereading Early Modern Race," *Shakespeare Quarterly* 67.1, 13. In this excerpt, the authors quote, first, Nada Elia, David M. Hernández, Jodi Kim, Shana L. Redmond, Dylan Rodriguez, and Sarita Eaxchavez See, "Introduction: A Sightline," in *Critical Ethnic Studies: A Reader* (Durham, NC: Duke UP, 2016), 3; and, secondly, Thompson, *Passing Strange*, 7–19.

14 Kim F. Hall, "I Can't Love You the Way You Want Me To: Archival Blackness." www.youtube.com/watch?v=szUlxHjUCOg (Begins at the 1:01.00 mark).

15 Ibid.

16 Ibid.

17 Ibid.

18 See, for example, Katherine Goodland, *Female Mourning in Medieval and Renaissance English Drama: From the Raising of Lazarus to King Lear* (Burlington, VT: Ashgate, 2005).

19 Fernando Orejuela, "Introduction," *Black Lives Matter and Music: Protest, Intervention, Reflection*, eds. Fernando Orejuela and Stephanie Shonekan (Bloomington, IN: Indiana UP, 2018): 1.

20 Kendrick Lamar, "Alright," from *To Pimp a Butterfly* (June 30, 2015). www.youtube.com/watch?v=Z-48u_uWMHY&index=656&list=PLw HlqcGmk6B2cdKspORZkk01fuuQI83DT

21 Ibid.

22 Ta-Nehisi Coates, *Between the World and Me* (New York: Spiegel and Grau, 2015): 10.

23 Ibid., 11–12.

24 See, for example, Oscar J. Martinez, Kathleen Staudt, Carmen E. Rodriguez, and Rosemary Neill, *Who Rules El Paso?: Private Gain, Public Policy, and the Community Interest* (El Paso, TX: Community First Coalition, 2020).

25 Baldwin, *Notes of a Native Son*, 115.

26 Luis Alberto Urrea, *The Devil's Highway* (New York: Little, Brown, and Company, 2004): 234.

27 Ibid., 234–5.

28 Ibid., 235.

Afterword

In early March of 2020, I returned home after a wonderful visit to Arizona State University where I had just given a talk—on material from this book in fact. At that time, speculation about the severity of the COVID-19 outbreak continued to grow in the United States. We were finally being told the truth about this virus and knew that this was going to be nothing like the flu. I was continuing work on this book at the time and on track to complete it before the summer months arrived. However, shortly after arriving back in El Paso, we swiftly went into a shutdown.

Like many people, I was paralyzed when it came to writing and continuing my research. We pivoted (and I will say it was a hard pivot) to online teaching, and we navigated the reality that things were not going to be normal for some time. In our household, we navigated the reality of sheltering in place and the reality that childcare was impossible. My plans for finishing the book before the summer flew out the window, and amid the many social media posts I read that boasted of bread baking, flourishing gardens, and home improvement projects, I saw that so many of my friends and colleagues were in a similar state of being when it came to concentrating on work. I felt it impossible. I could not get a handle on how surreal the world seemed to me. I know I am not alone in this. As I write this, we are eight months or so into this pandemic, and it still feels jarring at times, especially as the COVID-19 cases begin to surge both locally and worldwide. My intention here is not to make excuses for the delay in completing this book, but rather to contextualize where I was in my thinking and in regard to this project when the world shifted.

On May 25, 2020, George Floyd was murdered by Minneapolis police officers in the light of day and in full view for the world to behold. Floyd had paid for cigarettes with a counterfeit twenty-dollar bill, and the store employee made the decision to call the police. Approximately seventeen minutes after the police arrived, Floyd was dead.[1] He was unarmed. He did not resist arrest. He was handcuffed, lying face down on the ground with two officers unnecessarily holding his legs and another kneeling on his neck when he was killed. What the world witnessed was nothing short of a modern-day lynching, with the full force of bravado and the savagery of white supremacy behind it.

When I first heard the news, I was not surprised to learn that another unarmed Black man had been murdered by police, because unfortunately, and as this book outlines, such acts of police violence against Blacks are recursive. However, and like many other people, when I saw the video of his murder, I could barely comprehend the level of inhumanity that was there for everyone to see. I recognized the unmistakable evil behind the eyes of Derek Chauvin, the police officer who killed George Floyd. It is a casual and confident evil that unashamedly makes known the viciousness of white supremacy. Chauvin kept his knee on the neck of George Floyd for eight minutes and forty-six seconds. Eight minutes and forty-six seconds. Even when witnesses began filming the murder with their phones, Chauvin did not relent. Witnesses told Chauvin that he was going to kill him, and George Floyd himself said, "I'm about to die."[2] Still, he did not relent. It was clear that Chauvin was set on killing this Black man, and it was clear that his fellow officers on the scene allowed him to do it. It is excruciating to hear George Floyd repeat, "I can't breathe," again and again.[3] It is reminiscent of Eric Garner's last words when he was killed by police in New York City. It is excruciating to hear Floyd call for his mother when it is clear that he understands that he is about to die. His desperation is palpable. All the while, and with the full weight of his whiteness, Chauvin knelt on the neck of George Floyd until he killed him.

The act of kneeling—an act that until recently registered for many Colin Kaepernick's protest against police brutality—took on a different meaning in the summer of 2020. Indeed, in a summer when many COVID-19 victims were dying because they could not breathe, the actual words, "I can't breathe," were once again infused with such horrific valence. The murder of George Floyd contained within it a world of pain and anger. To be clear, many other unarmed Black men and women had also been killed in close temporal proximity to George Floyd—Breonna Taylor, Ahmaud Arbery, and Tony McDade all come to mind. But something about the sinister look on Chauvin's face took the world to its tipping point. All those killings, and the unending history of anti-Blackness, vicious racism, and boldfaced murder led to this watershed moment.

The protests that erupted worldwide after the murder of George Floyd, despite the global pandemic, was the kind of collective resistance to systemic racism that so many had been waiting so long to see. The Black Lives Matter movement—a movement that had not gone dormant—was magnified and suddenly it seemed that so many people finally understood the gravity behind those words. So many people recognized what many of us already knew about systemic racism in our nation. So many people said, with sincere belief, that we should defund the police. Major corporations, universities and colleges around the nation, professional sports teams, athletes, celebrities, politicians, and world leaders released statements to condemn the murder of George Floyd, to address anti-Blackness, and to say that Black lives matter. I readily recognize that for many of these entities, and indeed for many who expressed solidarity on social media, this was merely virtue signaling. Still, in a broader context, it meant that people were engaging—whether they wanted to or not—in conversations about the destructive effects of anti-Blackness and racism in our society. Like so many in our nation, I was glued to the television taking in the massive scope of the protests. It was a poignant moment, and, despite some media attempts to cast the protestors as looters and criminals, what the world saw was people finally coming together in solidarity to say that Black lives need to matter.

When George Floyd was murdered and the protests erupted, this book was mostly written (with various chapters in various states of disarray). It was clear to me that if I wanted to address the effect that the murder of George Floyd had on our society's attention to racism, I would have to commit to revisions that would result in a massive overhaul of the book. Of more importance, all of it felt too fresh, too raw, for me to process. In fact, it still does. While some misguided attempts to put the current tenor of the Black Lives Matter movement after the murder of George Floyd into conversation with Shakespeare emerged, I personally felt uneasy about trivializing such a profoundly important moment by inserting Shakespeare into that conversation. In the thick of those protests, it was a time for all of us who are not Black to step back and listen. I sought advice from friends in the field invested in critical race studies of Shakespeare, and taking their advice, I ultimately decided to finish the book I originally envisioned and add an afterword to address the current state of events. So, here I am—uneasy, unsure, and uncomfortable as I try to make sense of it all.

You see, the problem is that the energies behind the protests and the fact that so many people in our nation and across the world were paying attention gave me sincere hope. Yes, I did say "problem." When it comes to the issue of racism in our world, that kind of hope is hard to come by, and one often feels naïve to believe that things might actually change. And yet that is precisely what I felt. On a vast global scale, so many people seemed to get it. Statues of Confederate soldiers came down, building named after slave owners were renamed, and many were finally reckoning with our nation's racist history. In my hometown, both an elementary school and a street named after Robert E. Lee (truly, a sad stretch of road) were renamed. In the grand scheme of what was happening around the world, these symbolic acts might seem trivial. But they demonstrated that change was possible. I will readily admit that I felt energized.

As the excitement of the summer came to a close, and as it became clear that the pandemic was going to persist at least through the end of the year, the numbers of COVID-19 deaths continued to rise. Trump and his cronies had politicized the wearing of masks, the calls for social distancing, and the care that it takes to prevent the virus from spreading. He led from a position of irresponsibility, and people irresponsibly followed his lead. Everyone knew it was going to get very, very bad. For me, a sense of dread began to set in, and I quickly realized that it wasn't only the virus that made me uneasy, but the looming elections were making me very, very nervous.

This is why feeling hope in the summer felt like a problem to me. This is why I felt so strange to believe that things would be different. In my heart I knew that Trump had a very good chance of being reelected despite how unfavorably he was polling. We had been here before. We had all said, "they'll never elect him." We underestimated them. And we shouldn't, should we? The look on Chauvin's face came to mind. All the mask-less Trump supporters at his rallies reminded me of the extensive reach of racism. Nothing in this nation felt safe.

On some level, I recognized that this is the point—to keep us feeling unsafe. We know for a fact that COVID-19 disproportionally affects communities of color. As Daniel Wood writes:

> Today, as the U.S. has surpassed 200,000 COVID-19 deaths, and reached nearly 7 million confirmed cases, racial data is more complete, and the trend is crystal clear: People of color get sick and die of COVID-19 at rates higher than whites and higher than their share of the population.
>
> This trend has persisted—and in some cases worsened—since NPR analyzed this data in May. As the country struggles to bring the pandemic under control, Blacks, Latinos and Native Americans bear an unequal burden.[4]

I certainly believe that the ineptitude of the Trump administration is the primary reason why the number of COVID-19 infections and deaths are so extraordinarily high in the United States. However, given the track record of the Trump administration, I also believe that they are deliberately avoiding taking the necessary steps to get the virus under control because of the way it disproportionately affects people of color. This is an administration willing to separate children from their families at the U.S. Mexico border. This is an administration willing to perform forced sterilization surgeries on immigrant women. This is an administration to which the white supremacist Steve Bannon once belonged and to which the white supremacist Stephen Miller still belongs. You don't think they know and relish in the fact that the virus is killing more Black and brown people than anyone else? I feel that Carol Anderson's notion of white rage is particularly germane here. It is a sinister administration, and there is zero reason to believe they care.

All of this, then, brings me to this present moment. The book is written. Only this afterword remains. As I write this, it is almost two weeks since Joe Biden and Kamala Harris were elected to the Office of President and Vice President of the United States. Like many of you, I was on pins and needles for nearly five days as I waited for major networks to call the election. When the dust settled, the Biden-Harris ticket had flipped a number of states including Georgia and Arizona. There was reason to celebrate. It is not lost on me that the first woman elected to the Office of Vice President is a woman of color (Black and South Asian). It is not lost on me that Black women voters were the driving force in making sure Trump was not reelected. It is not lost on me that Latinx and Indigenous voters played a large role in flipping Arizona. And it certainly is not lost on me that white women voters turned out in higher numbers than in the 2016 election to, once again, vote for Trump.[5] Although 81 million Americans voted for Biden in this record-breaking election year, roughly 74 million Americans voted for Trump.

Those numbers ought to give us pause. Some 74 million Americans had no qualms about voting for a man who has consistently shown his racism, misogyny, and xenophobia to the American people. Some 74 million Americans voted for a man who put into effect a program meant to separate migrant children from their parents. Some 74 million Americans voted for a man who called on the Proud Boys—a white supremacist organization—to "stand back and stand by."[6] Those who voted for Trump knowingly voted for someone who is a known racist and who allowed our nation to put brown kids in cages. There is no other side here. They are comfortable with supporting these vile policies, and they are comfortable knowing that people of color would continue to suffer under his administration. Thankfully, as I write this, his days in office are numbered.

However, those voters remain, and their investment in systems of white supremacy is clearly in place. There is no doubt that Trump will seek to rally his base and perhaps attempt a run once again in 2024. What lies ahead is anyone's guess. In this moment, though, we need to sit with those high numbers, we need to recognize that so many of the citizens of this nation are willing to support violent racism, and we need, most of all, to be ready. There is nothing more urgent in our present moment than coming together to promote antiracist efforts.

We saw so many come out in large numbers in 2020 to remind us that Black lives matter. We saw the better (the best, in fact) part of the nation come out in full force to resist paradigms of white supremacy. And indeed, if we are looking for a silver lining, more American voters were not okay with the racism of the Trump administration. We won, but the fight is far from over. We have witnessed a paradigm shift, and

I firmly believe that for those of us committed to antiracist efforts, our time is now.

NOTES

1 Evan Hill, Ainara Tiefenthäler, Christian Triebert, Drew Jordan, Haley Willis, and Robin Stein, "How George Floyd Was Killed in Police Custody," *New York Times*, May 31, 2020. www.nytimes.com/2020/05/31/us/george-floyd-investigation.html

2 Jelani Cobb, "The Death of George Floyd, In Context," *The New Yorker*, May 28, 2020. www.newyorker.com/news/daily-comment/the-death-of-george-floyd-in-context

3 Ibid.

4 Daniel Wood, "As Pandemic Deaths Add Up, Racial Disparities Persist—And In Some Cases Worsen," NPR, September 23, 2020. www.npr.org/sections/health-shots/2020/09/23/914427907/as-pandemic-deaths-add-up-racial-disparities-persist-and-in-some-cases-worsen

5 See Jenn M. Jackson, "Yes, 55 Percent of White Women Voted for Trump. No, I'm Not Surprised," *Truthout*, November 14, 2020. https://truthout.org/articles/yes-55-percent-of-white-women-voted-for-trump-no-im-not-surprised/

6 Derek Hawkins, Cleve R. Wootson Jr., and Craig Timberg, "Trump's 'Stand By' Remark Puts the Proud Boys in the Spotlight," *The Washington Post*, September 30, 2020. www.washingtonpost.com/nation/2020/09/30/proudboys1001/

Further reading

The vibrant, varied, and extensive work on race studies of Shakespeare and early modern literature is impressive, and thus having to underscore only a handful of these works is the unenviable position in which I find myself. What is excluded is certainly as important as what is included, and as such my first suggestion here is that readers look to engage with critical race studies of Shakespeare and early modern literature beyond the parameters of this book. I will highlight several works that, to my mind, offer a compelling entry point to understanding precisely why race studies is the future of Shakespeare studies, but by no means is this at all comprehensive. I will not work chronologically here, but I will note that the area of race and Shakespeare has a history that is at least half a century old. What I offer is merely a snapshot of works that, I hope, will open the door to readers interested in learning more about this subject matter.

The works of two scholars—Margo Hendricks and Kim F. Hall—stand out to me at the outset, because their contributions to race studies of Shakespeare have been and continue to be instrumental to the shaping of our field. Hendricks' early collaboration with Patricia Parker in *Women, Race, and Writing in the Early Modern Period* (New York: Routledge, 1993) established her as a force, and her work thereafter continues to impress at every turn. Similarly, Kim F. Hall's landmark work, *Things of Darkness: Economies of Race and Gender in Early Modern England* (Ithaca, NY: Cornell UP, 1995), remains an impressively relevant exploration of constructions of race in early modern England and, to my mind, there is no other work that has been quite as influential to race studies of Shakespeare as this one. To that end, read it, and read it again.

I cannot overstate the influence that Ayanna Thompson has had on our field. She has, without doubt, paved the road to the future of Shakespeare studies at large. Her work, *Passing Strange: Shakespeare, Race, and Contemporary America* (Oxford: Oxford UP, 2013), broadened our understandings not only of Shakespeare but also of the way we think about cultural studies and the implications of focusing on race in our scholarly field. Her activist energies energized a whole generation of Shakespeare scholars. Her various edited collections bring manifold voices into our field, and most recently, her collection, *The Cambridge Companion to Shakespeare and Race* (Cambridge: Cambridge UP, 2021), offers work from scholars like Patricia Akhimie, Dennis Britton, Urvashi Chakravarty, Ambereen Dadabhoy, Miles Grier, Farah Karim-Cooper, Noémie Ndiaye, Melissa Sanchez, and Sandra Young, among others. I highlight these contributors to that collection because a quick search into their works will reveal to you a rich and exciting body of criticism on early modern race studies. The works of two contributors to that collection have also had a vital influence on our field—Joyce Green MacDonald, author of *Women and Race and Early Modern Texts* (Cambridge: Cambridge UP, 2010) and *Shakespearean Adaptation, Race and Memory in the New World* (New York: Palgrave 2020), and Arthur Little, author of *Shakespeare Jungle Fever: National-Imperial Re-Visions of Race, Rape, and Sacrifice* (Stanford: Stanford

UP, 2000). Both of these scholars maintain a prominent place in our field for good reason.

Perhaps no other singular essay stands out to me as instrumental reading for anyone interested in race and Shakespeare than Ian Smith's "Othello's Black Handkerchief" (*Shakespeare Quarterly* 64.1, 2013: 1–25). In this article, Smith is masterful in his ability to articulate—in ways that skillfully employ methodologies of several prominent sub-areas of our field— why attention to race matters. It is not hyperbole to say that this essay is perfectly executed, and as such I encourage everyone to read it. Smith's wider body of work will not disappoint either.

There are two special issues in major journals that I think are significant to studies of race and Shakespeare. The first is the *Shakespeare Quarterly* special collection on race and Shakespeare guest edited by Peter Erickson and Kim F. Hall (*Shakespeare Quarterly* 67.1, 2016). It is fitting that these two leaders in the field of Shakespeare and race were responsible for making this collection, the first of its kind in our field's flagship journal, possible. The second is the special issue, "Shakespeare and Black America," guest edited by Patricia Cahill and Kim F. Hall for *Journal of American Studies* (54, 2020). In addition to many of the scholars I have already mentioned, these two special issues feature work by, among others, Vanessa Corredera, Eric L. De Barros, Kyle Grady, Nedda Mehdizadeh, and Laura Lehua Yim. The work produced by these scholars is definitely worth your time.

We are also indebted to Bernadette Andrea, who offers us a rich body of criticism that examines the intersections of early modern literature and Islam. Jyotsna Singh and Ania Loomba have infused our field with important works on postcolonialism and race. The late Imtiaz Habib's *Black*

Lives in the English Archives, 1500–1677: Imprints of the Invisible (New York: Routledge, 2007) offers readers an understanding of the fact that there was a viable Black presence in early modern England. His work allows us to recognize the active resistance of an academy that, for so long, did not want to think about race or racism and, of more importance, Habib's work forces them to recognize that they cannot continue to ignore Black lives. Imtiaz will be sorely missed in our field. May he rest in power.

Clearly, I am struggling to bring this to an end, but it is only because such important work continues to be produced. If anything, I hope all of this illustrates that the area of early modern race studies is far from a niche field. It is a fully realized area of study that is defining how we think about Shakespeare, early modern literature, our academy, and our world at large. The work will continue to have a profound impact not only because the struggle continues but also because so many, I wholeheartedly believe, are recognizing the importance of joining in that struggle.

Index